HISTORIC DOCUMENTS
OF WORLD WAR II

WALTER CONSUELO LANGSAM

President
University of Cincinnati

AN ANVIL ORIGINAL
under the general editorship of
LOUIS L. SNYDER

909.82

D. VAN NOSTRAND COMPANY, INC.
PRINCETON, NEW JERSEY
TORONTO   LONDON
NEW YORK

ST. BONAVENTURE LIBRARY
ST. BONAVENTURE, N. Y.

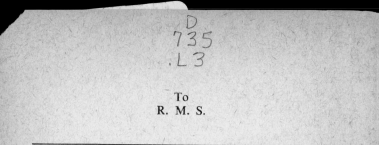

To
R. M. S.

D
735
.L3

D. VAN NOSTRAND COMPANY, INC.

120 Alexander St., Princeton, New Jersey (*Principal office*)
257 Fourth Avenue, New York 10, New York
25 Hollinger Rd., Toronto 16, Canada
358, Kensington High Street, London, W.14, England

COPYRIGHT, ©, 1958, BY
WALTER CONSUELO LANGSAM
Published simultaneously in Canada by
D. Van Nostrand Company (Canada), Ltd.

No reproduction in any form of this book, in whole or in part (except for brief quotation in critical articles or reviews), may be made without written authorization from the publishers.

Library of Congress Catalog Card No. 58-14435

PRINTED IN THE UNIT̲ ̲RICA

394598

OCT 25 '84
MAY 19 '90

PREFACE

During a time in which not only every student but every
man and woman must have certain background information in order to understand the day's news and evaluate
the policies and actions of a democratic government, it is
essential that there be available, in brief form, certain basic
source materials concerning the outbreak, conduct, and
aftermath of World War II. An effort has been made in
this slim volume to provide some such material. The list
includes treaties, pacts, laws, decrees, governmental acts,
armistices, examples of official propaganda, conventions,
authoritative narrative descriptions of special incidents,
and the like. The introductory lines preceding each document are intended to provide a useful frame of reference
and furnish relevant information not always easy of access. The footnote references are designed to establish the
authenticity of the quoted material and to acquaint the
reader with a variety of available primary sources.

WALTER C. LANGSAM

Cincinnati, Ohio
January, 1958

TABLE OF CONTENTS

THE NAMING OF WORLD WAR II, SEPTEMBER 11, 1945 [1]

There was much discussion in the United States during the early 1940's regarding an appropriate name for the war that began with the German invasion of Poland in 1939. On September 11, 1945, the United States Government officially adopted the title "World War II" through a joint letter signed by the secretaries of war and of the navy, and approved by President Harry S. Truman.

↗   ↗   ↗

10 September 1945

The President
The White House

Dear Mr. President:

President Wilson, under date of July 31, 1919, addressed a letter to Secretary of War Baker which read, in part, as follows:

"It is hard to find a satisfactory 'official' name for the war, but the best, I think, that has been suggested is 'The World War,' and I hope that your judgment will concur."

Subsequently, under date of October 7, 1919, War Department General Orders No. 115 directed:

"The war against the Central Powers of Europe, in which the United States has taken part, will hereafter be designated in all official communications and publications as 'The World War.'"

As a matter of simplicity and to insure uniform terminology, it is recommended that "World War II" be the

[1] United States, Department of State, *Bulletin* (Government Printing Office, Washington, 1945), XIII, 427-428.

officially designated name for the present war covering all theaters and the entire period of hostilities.

The term "World War II" has been used in at least seven public laws to designate this period of hostilities. Analysis of publications and radio programs indicates that this term has been accepted by common usage.

If this recommendation is approved it is further recommended that the title "World War II" be published in the *Federal Register* as the official name of the present war. [See 10 *Federal Register* 1188.]

Respectfully yours,
HENRY L. STIMSON,
Secretary of War

JAMES FORRESTAL,
  Secretary of the Navy.

Approved: September 11, 1945
  HARRY S. TRUMAN

— 2 —

HITLER'S DECREE ON COMMAND OF THE WEHRMACHT, FEBRUARY 4, 1938 [2]

In the period from 1935 to 1938, certain leaders of the High Command of the Armed Forces fell into Chancellor Adolf Hitler's bad graces. Some of these generals were not members of the Nazi Party. Some, with a Prussian Junker background, despised the activities of the former corporal who now called himself Fuehrer. Some felt their Christian sympathies outraged by the religious policies of the Third Reich. And some disapproved of the seemingly reckless military and foreign policies of Hitler—policies

[2] Germany, *Reichsministerium des Innern, Reichsgesetzblatt,* 1938, pt. I, p. 111.

which they felt could only plunge Germany into a war for which she was not ready. Aware of this situation, and looking ahead to further bold foreign measures, Hitler early in 1938 dismissed some of the top military leaders and subordinated the High Command directly to his own control. Thus prepared, Hitler planned his successive aggressions against Czechoslovakia, Austria, and Poland.

✓   ✓   ✓

As of now, I am personally assuming direct command of the entire Wehrmacht.

The former Department of the Wehrmacht in the Reich Ministry of War, with all its assignments, comes directly under my command as the High Command of the Wehrmacht and as my military staff.

The former Chief of the Department of the Wehrmacht becomes Chief of Staff of the High Command of the Wehrmacht with the title "Chief of the High Command of the Wehrmacht." His rank is equivalent to that of a Reich Minister.

The High Command of the Wehrmacht assumes control of the affairs of the Reich Ministry of War; the Chief of the Wehrmacht exercises, in my name, the authority hitherto vested in the Reich Minister of War.

The obligation of the High Command of the Wehrmacht in time of peace is the unified preparation in all spheres of the defense of the Reich according to my directives.

Berlin, 4 February 1938
The Fuehrer and Reich Chancellor: ADOLF HITLER

— 3 —

THE MUNICH AGREEMENT, SEPTEMBER 29, 1938[3]

For a time in 1938 it appeared that Nazi Germany's demands concerning the Sudetenland and other parts of Czechoslovakia inhabited by German-speaking people might lead to war. On the initiative of Prime Minister Neville Chamberlain, a "last-minute" conference was held in Munich among the premiers of Great Britain, France, Germany, and Italy. The resulting Munich Agreement temporarily averted war by the "appeasement" of Chancellor Adolf Hitler. Germany was given, without battle, virtually all that she had demanded under threat of war. "Munich" thus became a popular synonym for appeasement.

✓   ✓   ✓

A. Personal Message Sent by the Prime Minister [Neville Chamberlain] to the Reichschancellor on September 28, 1938

After reading your letter I feel certain that you can get all essentials without war and without delay.

I am ready to come to Berlin myself at once to discuss arrangements for transfer with you and representatives of Czech Government, together with representatives of France and Italy if you desire.

I feel convinced we could reach agreement in a week. However much you distrust Prague Government's intentions, you cannot doubt power of British and French Gov-

[3] Great Britain, *Further Documents Respecting Czechoslovakia, Including the Agreement Concluded at Munich on September 29, 1938. Presented by the Secretary of State for Foreign Affairs to Parliament by Command of His Majesty*, Misc. No. 8 (1938), Cmd. 5848 (His Majesty's Stationery Office, London, 1938), pp. 2, 3-6.

ernments to see that promises are carried out fairly and fully and forthwith. As you know I have stated publicly that we are prepared to undertake that they shall be so carried out.

I cannot believe that you will take responsibility of starting a world war which may end civilisation for the sake of a few days' delay in settling this long-standing problem.

B. AGREEMENT CONCLUDED AT MUNICH ON SEPTEMBER 29, 1938

Germany, the United Kingdom, France, and Italy, taking into consideration the agreement, which has been already reached in principle for the cession to Germany of the Sudeten German territory, have agreed on the following terms and conditions governing the said cession and the measures consequent thereon, and by this agreement they each hold themselves responsible for the steps necessary to secure its fulfilment :—

1. The evacuation will begin on the 1st October.

2. The United Kingdom, France, and Italy agree that the evacuation of the territory shall be completed by the 10th October, without any existing installations having been destroyed and that the Czechoslovak Government will be held responsible for carrying out the evacuation without damage to the said installations.

3. The conditions governing the evacuation will be laid down in detail by an international commission composed of representatives of Germany, the United Kingdom, France, Italy, and Czechoslovakia.

4. The occupation by stages of the predominantly German territory by German troops will begin on the 1st October. The four territories marked on the attached map will be occupied by German troops in the following order : the territory marked No. I on the 1st and 2nd of October, the territory marked No. II on the 2nd and 3rd of October, the territory marked No. III on the 3rd, 4th, and 5th of October, the territory marked No. IV on the 6th and 7th of October. The remaining territory of preponderantly German character will be ascertained by the aforesaid international commission forthwith and be occupied by German troops by the 10th of October.

5. The international commission referred to in para-

graph 3 will determine the territories in which a plebiscite is to be held. These territories will be occupied by international bodies until the plebiscite has been completed. The same commission will fix the conditions in which the plebiscite is to be held, taking as a basis the conditions of the Saar plebiscite. The commission will also fix a date, not later than the end of November, on which the plebiscite will be held.

6. The final determination of the frontiers will be carried out by the international commission. This commission will also be entitled to recommend to the four Powers, Germany, the United Kingdom, France, and Italy, in certain exceptional cases minor modifications in the strictly ethnographical determination of the zones which are to be transferred without plebiscite.

7. There will be a right of option into and out of the transferred territories, the option to be exercised within six months from the date of this agreement. A German-Czechoslovak commission shall determine the details of the option, consider ways of facilitating the transfer of population and settle questions of principle arising out of the said transfer.

8. The Czechoslovak Government will within a period of four weeks from the date of this agreement release from their military and police forces any Sudeten Germans who may wish to be released, and the Czechoslovak Government will within the same period release Sudeten German prisoners who are serving terms of imprisonment for political offences.

ADOLF HITLER
NEVILLE CHAMBERLAIN
ÉDOUARD DALADIER
BENITO MUSSOLINI

Munich,
September 29, 1938

ANNEX TO THE AGREEMENT

His Majesty's Government in the United Kingdom and the French Government have entered into the above agreement on the basis that they stand by the offer, contained in paragraph 6 of the Anglo-French proposals of the 19th September [Cmd. 5847] relating to an international guar-

antee of the new boundaries of the Czechoslovak State
against unprovoked aggression.

When the question of the Polish and Hungarian minorities in Czechoslovakia has been settled, Germany and Italy
for their part will give a guarantee to Czechoslovakia.

DECLARATION

The Heads of the Governments of the four Powers
declare that the problems of the Polish and Hungarian
minorities in Czechoslovakia, if not settled within three
months by agreement between the respective Governments shall form the subject of another meeting of the
Heads of the Governments of the four Powers here present.

SUPPLEMENTARY DECLARATION

All questions which may arise out of the transfer of the
territory shall be considered as coming within the terms of
reference to the international commission.

COMPOSITION OF THE INTERNATIONAL COMMISSION

The four Heads of Government here present agree that
the international commission provided for in the agreement signed by them today, shall consist of the Secretary
of State in the German Foreign Office, the British, French,
and Italian Ambassadors accredited in Berlin, and a representative to be nominated by the Government of Czechoslovakia.

Munich,
   September 29, 1938

— 4 —

THE WESTERN GUARANTEE OF POLISH INDEPENDENCE, MARCH 31, 1939 [4]

In March, 1939, the Nazi Government aimed its propaganda guns at Danzig and the Polish Corridor, which had been part of Germany before the Versailles Treaty. Having learned from past experience that this presaged Nazi aggression against Poland, the governments in London and Paris promised to aid the Poles if these used force to resist a threat to their independence. Poland on April 6 accepted this guarantee as a mutual obligation.

✓   ✓   ✓

The Prime Minister (Mr. Chamberlain): The right hon. gentleman the leader of the Opposition asked me this morning whether I could make a statement as to the European situation. As I said this morning, His Majesty's Government have no official confirmation of the rumours of any projected attack on Poland and they must not, therefore, be taken as accepting them as true.

I am glad to take this opportunity of stating again the general policy of His Majesty's Government. They have constantly advocated the adjustment, by way of free negotiation between the parties concerned, of any differences that may arise between them. They consider that this is the natural and proper course where differences exist. In their opinion there should be no question incapable of solu-

[4] Great Britain, *Documents Concerning German-Polish Relations and the Outbreak of Hostilities between Great Britain and Germany on September 3, 1939. Presented by the Secretary of State for Foreign Affairs to Parliament by Command of His Majesty,* Misc. No. 9 (1939), Cmd. 6106 (His Majesty's Stationery Office, London, 1939), p. 36.

tion by peaceful means, and they would see no justification for the substitution of force or threats of force for the method of negotiation.

As the House is aware, certain consultations are now proceeding with other Governments. In order to make perfectly clear the position of His Majesty's Government in the meantime before those consultations are concluded, I now have to inform the House that during that period, in the event of any action which clearly threatened Polish independence, and which the Polish Government accordingly considered it vital to resist with their national forces, His Majesty's Government would feel themselves bound at once to lend the Polish Government all support in their power. They have given the Polish Government an assurance to this effect.

I may add that the French Government have authorised me to make it plain that they stand in the same position in this matter as do His Majesty's Government.

— 5 —

THE ITALO-GERMAN ALLIANCE, MAY 22, 1939 [5]

Some years after World War I, Fascist Italy became the leader of a "revisionist bloc" which sought to modify the Peace of Paris (1919-1920) in favor of its members. Under Chancellor Adolf Hitler, Germany became the leader of this bloc—a circumstance which Premier Benito Mussolini in effect recognized after the successful Nazi aggression against Austria in 1938. Little more than a year later, Berlin and Rome signed an alliance. The "Se-

[5] *Völkischer Beobachter,* May 23, 1939.

cret Supplementary Protocol" was not known in the West until after the defeat of the Axis Powers.

✓   ✓   ✓

The German Reich Chancellor and His Majesty the King of Italy and Albania, Emperor of Ethiopia, consider that the time has come to confirm through a solemn pact the close relation of friendship and affinity which exists between National Socialist Germany and Fascist Italy.

Since a secure bridge for mutual help and assistance has been established through the common boundary between Germany and Italy, fixed for all time, the two Governments acknowledge anew the principles and aims of the policy previously agreed upon by them, and which has shown itself successful in furthering the interests of the two countries as well as in ensuring the peace of Europe.

Firmly bound together through the inner unity of their ideologies and the comprehensive solidarity of their interests, the German and the Italian people are determined also in future to stand side by side and to strive with united effort for the securing of their *Lebensraum* [living space] and the maintenance of peace.

In this way, prescribed for them by history, Germany and Italy wish, in a world of unrest and disintegration, to carry out the assignment of making safe the foundations of European culture.

In order to establish these principles in treaty form, they have named as plenipotentiaries, the German Reich Chancellor, the Minister of Foreign Affairs, von Ribbentrop, His Majesty the King of Italy and Albania, Emperor of Ethiopia, the Minister of Foreign Affairs, Count Galeazzo Ciano, who, after the exchange of proper credentials, have agreed upon the following terms:

ARTICLE I. The Contracting Parties will remain in permanent contact with each other, in order to come to an understanding of all common interests or the European situation as a whole.

ARTICLE II. In the event that the common interests of the Contracting Parties be jeopardized through international happenings of any kind, they will immediately enter into consultation regarding the necessary measures to preserve these interests.

Should the security or other vital interests of one of the Contracting Parties be threatened from outside, the other

Contracting Party will afford the threatened Party its full political and diplomatic support in order to remove this threat.

ARTICLE III. If it should happen, against the wishes and hopes of the Contracting Parties, that one of them becomes involved in military complications with another Power or other Powers, the other Contracting Party will immediately step to its side as an ally and will support it with all its military might on land, at sea, and in the air.

ARTICLE IV. In order to ensure, in any given case, the rapid implementation of the alliance obligations of Article III, the Governments of the two Contracting Parties will further intensify their cooperation in the military sphere and the sphere of war economy.

Similarly the two Governments will keep each other regularly informed of other measures necessary for the practical implementation of this pact.

The two Governments will create standing commissions, under the direction of the Foreign Ministers, for the purposes indicated in paragraphs 1 and 2.

ARTICLE V. The Contracting Parties already at this point bind themselves, in the event of a jointly waged war, to conclude any armistice or peace only in full agreement with each other.

ARTICLE VI. The two Contracting Parties are aware of the importance of their joint relations to the Powers which are friendly to them. They are determined to maintain these relations in future and to promote the adequate development of the common interests which bind them to these Powers.

ARTICLE VII. This pact comes into force immediately upon its signing. The two Contracting Parties are agreed upon fixing the first period of its validity at ten years. In good time before the elapse of this period they will come to an agreement regarding the extension of the validity of the pact.

SECRET SUPPLEMENTARY PROTOCOL[6]

On signing the friendship and alliance pact, agreement

---

[6] The secret protocol is from United States, Office of United States Chief of Counsel for Prosecution of Axis Criminality, *Nazi Conspiracy and Aggression,* 8 vols. and 2 suppl. vols. (Government Printing Office, Washington, 1946-1948), V, 453, Doc. No. 2818-PS.

has been established by both parties on the following
points:

1. The two Foreign Ministers will as quickly as possible
come to an agreement on the organization, the seat, and
the methods of work on the pact of the commissions on
military questions and questions of war economy as stipulated in Article IV of the pact.

2. For the execution of Article IV, par. 2, the two
Foreign Ministers will as quickly as possible arrange the
necessary measures, guaranteeing a constant cooperation,
conforming to the spirit and aims of the pact, in matters of
the press, the news service and the propaganda. For this
purpose in particular, each of the two Foreign Ministers
will assign to the embassy of his country in the respective
capital one or several especially well-experienced special-
ists, for constant discussion in direct close cooperation
with the resp. Ministry of Foreign Affairs, of the suitable
steps to be taken in matters of the press, the news service,
and the propaganda for the promotion of the policy of the
Axis, and as a countermeasure against the policy of the
enemy powers.

*Berlin 22 May 1939 in the XVII year of the Fascist
Aera.*

— 6 —

THE GERMAN-SOVIET TREATY OF NON-AGGRESSION, AUGUST 23, 1939[7]

[7] United States, Department of State, Publication No. 3023,
*Nazi-Soviet Relations 1939-1941. Documents from the
Archives of the German Foreign Office* (Government
Printing Office, Washington, 1948), pp. 76-78.

The German and Soviet foreign ministers signed a ten-year non-aggression pact in Moscow at the very time when British and French officers were holding "military conversations" with their Soviet opposites. A "Secret Supplementary Protocol," first published in 1948, virtually carved Eastern Europe into German and Soviet spheres. (For a later revision of this protocol, see Document No. 9.) The pact was politically realistic for both signatories. Germany was relieved of worry regarding an eastern front if Great Britain and France helped Poland in case of a German attack. And the U.S.S.R. got both time to advance industrialization under the Third Five-Year Plan and German approval for her imperialistic designs against the Baltic States, Poland, and Romania.

✓   ✓   ✓

The Government of the German Reich and the Government of the Union of Soviet Socialist Republics desirous of strengthening the cause of peace between Germany and the U.S.S.R., and proceeding from the fundamental provisions of the Neutrality Agreement concluded in April 1926 between Germany and the U.S.S.R., have reached the following agreement:

ARTICLE I. Both High Contracting Parties obligate themselves to desist from any act of violence, any aggressive action, and any attack on each other, either individually or jointly with other powers.

ARTICLE II. Should one of the High Contracting Parties become the object of belligerent action by a third power, the other High Contracting Party shall in no manner lend its support to this third power.

ARTICLE III. The Governments of the two High Contracting Parties shall in the future maintain continual contact with one another for the purpose of consultation in order to exchange information on problems affecting their common interests.

ARTICLE IV. Neither of the two High Contracting Parties shall participate in any grouping of powers whatsoever that is directly or indirectly aimed at the other party.

ARTICLE V. Should disputes or conflicts arise between the High Contracting Parties over problems of one kind or another, both parties shall settle these disputes or conflicts exclusively through friendly exchange of opinion or, if necessary, though the establishment of arbitration commissions.

ARTICLE VI. The present treaty is concluded for a period of ten years, with the provision that, in so far as one of the High Contracting Parties does not denounce it one year prior to the expiration of this period, the validity of this treaty shall automatically be extended for another five years.

ARTICLE VII. The present treaty shall be ratified within the shortest possible time. The ratifications shall be exchanged in Berlin. The agreement shall enter into force as soon as it is signed.

Done in duplicate, in the German and Russian languages. Moscow, August 23, 1939

For the Government of the German Reich:	With full power of the Government of the U.S.S.R.:
v. RIBBENTROP	V. MOLOTOV

Secret Supplementary Protocol

On the occasion of the signature of the Non-Aggression Pact between the German Reich and the Union of Soviet Socialist Republics the undersigned plenipotentiaries of each of the two parties discussed in strictly confidential conversations the question of the boundary of their respective spheres of influence in Eastern Europe. These conversations led to the following conclusions:

1. In the event of a territorial and political rearrangement in the areas belonging to the Baltic States (Finland, Estonia, Latvia, Lithuania), the northern boundary of Lithuania shall represent the boundary of the spheres of influence of Germany and the U.S.S.R. In this connection the interest of Lithuania in the Vilna area is recognized by each party.

2. In the event of a territorial and political rearrangement of the areas belonging to the Polish state, the spheres of influence of Germany and the U.S.S.R. shall be bounded approximately by the line of the rivers Narew, Vistula, and San.

The question of whether the interests of both parties make desirable the maintenance of an independent Polish state and how such a state should be bounded can only be definitely determined in the course of further political developments. In any event both Governments will resolve this question by means of a friendly agreement.

3. With regard to Southeastern Europe attention is called by the Soviet side to its interest in Bessarabia. The German side declares its complete political disinterestedness in these areas.

4. This protocol shall be treated by both parties as strictly secret.

Moscow, August 23, 1939

For the Government	*Plenipotentiary of the*
of the German Reich:	*Government of the U.S.S.R.:*
v. RIBBENTROP	V. MOLOTOV

— 7 —

THE GERMAN ULTIMATUM TO POLAND, AUGUST 30-31, 1939[8]

Toward the end of August 1939, Chancellor Adolf Hitler was ready to invade Poland unless the latter gave up Danzig and the Polish Corridor voluntarily. Great Britain tried, as at the time of the Czechoslovak crisis (see Document No. 3), to substitute appeasement for war. But on

[8] German Library of Information, *Documents on the Events Preceding the Outbreak of the War. Compiled and Published by the German Foreign Office* (New York, 1940), pp. 485-488. A slightly different translation may be found in Great Britain, *Documents Concerning German-Polish Relations and the Outbreak of Hostilities between Great Britain and Germany on September 3, 1939. Presented by the Secretary of State for Foreign Affairs to Parliament by Command of His Majesty,* Misc. No. 9 (1939), Cmd. 6106 (His Majesty's Stationery Office, London, 1939), pp. 150-153.

*August 29, Germany asked London to induce Warsaw to
send a special Polish delegate to Berlin on August 30 with
full power to accept a settlement. On the thirtieth, the
British Ambassador to Germany suggested that the demands on Poland be transmitted through the customary
embassy channels. By way of reply, Foreign Minister
Joachim von Ribbentrop, at midnight of the thirtieth, read
to the British Ambassador, "at top speed," a sixteen-point
ultimatum for the resolution of Polish-German differences.
Only on the thirty-first, when the ultimatum was broad-
cast over the radio, was an official copy also handed to the
British Ambassador. And then the Nazis interpreted as a
Polish rejection of their peace proposals the fact that
Warsaw did not send to Berlin, on twenty-four hours'
notice, a representative empowered to accept an ultimatum
which the home government had not even seen.*

✦   ✦   ✦

The situation between the German Reich and Poland is
at the present time such that any further incident may lead
to an outbreak of hostilities between the military forces of
the two countries, which have already taken up their positions on their respective sides of the frontier. Any peaceful solution of the problem must be of such a nature that
the events which originally brought about this state of
affairs cannot be repeated on another occasion, thus caus-
ing a state of tension not only in Eastern Europe but also
elsewhere.

The causes of this development are to be found in (1)
the intolerable demarcation of the frontiers as dictated in
the Treaty of Versailles, (2) the intolerable treatment of
the minority in the territories cut off from the Reich.

In putting forward these proposals, the German Government are attempting to find a final solution, putting an
end to the intolerable situation arising from the present
demarcation of frontiers, securing to both parties their
vital lines of communication, eliminating as far as possible
the problem of the minorities and, insofar as this should
prove impossible, rendering the fate of the minorities bear-
able by effectively guaranteeing their rights.

The German Government feel convinced that it is indis-
pensable that economic and personal damage inflicted since

1918 should be investigated, and full compensation made therefor. Of course, the German Government regard this obligation as binding upon both parties.

The above considerations give rise to the following concrete proposals:

1. By reason of its purely German character and the unanimous will of its population, the Free City of Danzig shall be returned forthwith to the German Reich.

2. The territory known as the Polish Corridor, that is to say, the territory bounded by the Baltic Sea and a line running from Marienwerder to Graudenz, Kulm, Bromberg, (including these towns), and then in a westerly direction towards Schönlanke, shall itself decide whether it shall become part of the German Reich or remain with Poland.

3. For that purpose, a plebiscite shall be held in this territory. All Germans who were domiciled in this area on January 1, 1918, or who were born there on or before that day, and also all Poles, Cassubians, etc., who were domiciled in this area on that day or who were born there on or before the above-mentioned date, shall be entitled to vote. Germans who have been expelled from this territory shall return for the purpose of registering their votes.

In order to ensure an impartial plebiscite and to guarantee that the necessary and extensive preparations for the plebiscite shall be carried out correctly, an International Commission like the one formed in connection with the Saar plebiscite, and consisting of members appointed by the four Great Powers, Italy, the U.S.S.R., France, and Great Britain, shall be formed immediately, and placed in charge of this territory. This commission shall exercise sovereign rights throughout the territory. To that end, the territory shall be evacuated by the Polish military forces, by the Polish police, and by the Polish authorities within the shortest possible time to be agreed upon.

4. The Polish port of Gdynia to the extent of the Polish settlement is not included in this area, but, as a matter of principle, is recognized as Polish territory.

The details of the boundaries of this Polish port shall be decided on by Germany and Poland, and if necessary established by an International Court of Arbitration.

5. In order to allow for ample time for the necessary

and extensive preparations for the carrying out of an impartial plebiscite, this plebiscite shall not take place before a period of twelve months has elapsed.

6. In order that during that period, Germany's lines of communication with East Prussia and Poland's access to the sea may be unrestrictedly ensured, certain roads and railway lines shall be determined, in order to facilitate unobstructed transit. In this connection only such taxes may be levied as are necessary for the upkeep of the lines of communication and for the carrying out of transport.

7. The allocation of this territory shall be decided on by the absolute majority of the votes cast.

8. In order to secure, after the plebiscite (irrespective of the result thereof), Germany's unrestricted communication with the province of Danzig-East Prussia, and Poland's access to the sea, Germany shall, in case the territory be returned to Poland as a result of the plebiscite, be given an extraterritorial traffic zone running from, say, Bütow to Danzig or Dirschau, for the purpose of building a German motor highway (*Reichsautobahn*) and also a four-track railway line. The construction of the motor road and of the railway shall be carried out in such a manner that Polish lines of communication are not affected thereby, i.e., they are to be overbridged or underbridged. This zone shall be one kilometer in width and shall be German territory.

Should the result of the plebiscite be in favor of Germany, Poland shall have the same rights as Germany would have had, to build an extraterritorial road and railway connection in order to secure her free and unrestricted access to her port of Gdynia.

9. In the event of the Polish Corridor being returned to the Reich, the latter declares herself prepared to arrange with Poland for an exchange of population, insofar as conditions in the Corridor lend themselves to such an exchange.

10. Any special rights claimed by Poland within the port of Danzig shall be negotiated on a parity basis in exchange for equal rights for Germany at the Port of Gdynia.

11. In order to avoid any sense of menace or danger on either side, Danzig and Gdynia shall henceforth have a purely commercial character; i.e., neither of these places

shall be provided with means of military defense or fortifications.

12. The Peninsula of Hela, which according to the result of the plebiscite would be allocated either to Poland or to Germany, shall also be demilitarized in any case.

13. The German Government, having most serious complaints to make about the treatment of the minority by the Poles, and the Polish Government, considering themselves entitled to raise complaints against Germany, agree to investigate into all complaints about economic and personal damage, as well as other acts of terrorism.

Germany and Poland bind themselves to indemnify the minorities on either side for any economic damages and other wrongs inflicted upon them since 1918; and/or to revoke all expropriations or otherwise to completely indemnify the respective person or persons for these and other encroachments upon economic life.

14. In order to free the Germans remaining in Poland, as well as the Poles remaining in Germany, from the feeling of being deprived of the benefits of international law, and above all to afford them the certainty of their not being made to take part in actions and in furnishing services of a kind not compatible with their national convictions, Germany and Poland mutually agree to safeguard the rights of their respective minorities by most comprehensive and binding agreements for the purpose of warranting these minorities the preservation, free development and cultivation of their national customs, habits and traditions, to grant them in particular and for that purpose the form of organization considered necessary by them. Both parties undertake not to draft the members of the minority into military service.

15. In case of an agreement being reached on the basis of these proposals, Germany and Poland declare themselves prepared immediately to order and carry out the demobilization of their respective armed forces.

16. Any additional measures required to hasten the carrying through of the above agreement shall be mutually agreed upon between Germany and Poland.

ST. BONAVENTURE LIBRARY
ST. BONAVENTURE, N. Y.

— 8 —

THE BRITISH DECLARATION OF WAR ON GERMANY, SEPTEMBER 3, 1939 [9]

When Germany refused to withdraw the forces she had sent into Poland without warning on the night of August 31–September 1, 1939, Great Britain and France, on September 3, in accordance with their commitment of March 31, 1939 (see Document No. 4), *declared the existence of a state of war between themselves and the Nazis. The fact was made public by Prime Minister Neville Chamberlain in the House of Commons.*

✦   ✦   ✦

When I spoke last night to the House, I could not but be aware that in some parts of the House there were doubts and some bewilderment as to whether there had been any weakening, hesitation or vacillation on the part of His Majesty's Government. In the circumstances, I make no reproach, for if I had been in the same position as hon. members not sitting on this Bench and not in possession of all the information which we have, I should very likely have felt the same. The statement which I have to make this morning will show that there were no grounds for doubt. We were in consultation all day yesterday with the French Government, and we felt that the intensified action which the Germans were taking against Poland allowed no delay in making our own position clear. Accordingly, we decided to send to our Ambassador in Berlin instructions which he was to hand at nine o'clock this morning to the German Foreign Secretary and which read as follows:

[9] Great Britain, *Parliamentary Debates, House of Commons,* Fifth Series, CCCLI, 291–292.

"Sir,

In the communication which I had the honour to make to you on 1st September, I informed you, on the instructions of His Majesty's Principal Secretary of State for Foreign Affairs, that unless the German Government were prepared to give His Majesty's Government in the United Kingdom satisfactory assurances that the German Government had suspended all aggressive action against Poland and were prepared promptly to withdraw their forces from Polish territory, His Majesty's Government in the United Kingdom would, without hesitation, fulfil their obligations to Poland.

Although this communication was made more than 24 hours ago, no reply has been received, but German attacks upon Poland have been continued and intensified. I have, accordingly, the honour to inform you that unless not later than 11 A.M., British Summer Time, today September 3rd, satisfactory assurances to the above effect have been given by the German Government and have reached His Majesty's Government in London, a state of war will exist between the two countries as from that hour."

That was the final Note. No such undertaking was received by the time stipulated, and, consequently, this country is at war with Germany. I am in a position to inform the House that, according to arrangements made between the British and French Governments, the French Ambassador in Berlin is at this moment making a similar démarche, accompanied also by a definite time limit. The House has already been made aware of our plans. As I said the other day, we are ready.

This is a sad day for all of us, and to none is it sadder than to me. Everything that I have worked for, everything that I have hoped for, everything that I have believed in during my public life, has crashed into ruins. There is only one thing left for me to do; that is, to devote what strength and powers I have to forwarding the victory of the cause for which we have to sacrifice so much. I cannot tell what part I may be allowed to play myself; I trust I may live to see the day when Hitlerism has been destroyed and a liberated Europe has been re-established.

THE GERMAN-SOVIET BOUNDARY AGREEMENT, SEPTEMBER 28, 1939[10]

While the outmanned and outmaneuvered Poles were trying to make a stand against the Nazis in southern and eastern Poland, the Soviet Union on September 17, 1939, invaded the unhappy country. The official explanation was the protection of the Ukrainian and White Russian minorities living in eastern Poland. Berlin and Moscow promptly divided the spoils.

✓   ✓   ✓

The Government of the German Reich and the Government of the U.S.S.R. consider it as exclusively their task, after the collapse of the former Polish state, to re-establish peace and order in these territories and to assure to the peoples living there a peaceful life in keeping with their national character. To this end, they have agreed upon the following:

ARTICLE I. The Government of the German Reich and the Government of the U.S.S.R. determine as the boundary of their respective national interests in the territory of the former Polish state the line marked on the attached map, which shall be described in more detail in a supplementary protocol.

[10] United States, Department of State, Publication No. 3023, *Nazi-Soviet Relations 1939-1941. Documents from the Archives of the German Foreign Office* (Government Printing Office, Washington, 1948), pp. 105-108. The map and supplementary protocol referred to in Article I are not printed here. The German-Soviet boundary cut through the old Poland approximately along a line reaching from the southwestern tip of Lithuania to the northeastern edge of Hungary.

ARTICLE II. Both parties recognize the boundary of the respective national interests established in Article I as definitive and shall reject any interference of third powers in this settlement.

ARTICLE III. The necessary reorganization of public administration will be effected in the areas west of the line specified in Article I by the Government of the German Reich, in the areas east of this line by the Government of the U.S.S.R.

ARTICLE IV. The Government of the German Reich and the Government of the U.S.S.R. regard this settlement as a firm foundation for a progressive development of the friendly relations between their peoples.

ARTICLE V. This treaty shall be ratified and the ratifications shall be exchanged in Berlin as soon as possible. The treaty becomes effective upon signature.

Done in duplicate, in the German and Russian languages.

Moscow, September 28, 1939

For the Government	*By authority of the*
of the German Reich:	*Government of the U.S.S.R.:*
J. RIBBENTROP	V. MOLOTOV

CONFIDENTIAL PROTOCOL

The Government of the U.S.S.R. shall place no obstacles in the way of Reich nationals and other persons of German descent residing in the territories under its jurisdiction, if they desire to migrate to Germany or to the territories under German jurisdiction. It agrees that such removals shall be carried out by agents of the Government of the Reich in cooperation with the competent local authorities and that the property rights of the emigrants shall be protected.

A corresponding obligation is assumed by the Government of the German Reich in respect to the persons of Ukrainian or White Russian descent residing in the territories under its jurisdiction.

Moscow, September 28, 1939

For the Government	*By authority of the*
of the German Reich:	*Government of the U.S.S.R.:*
J. RIBBENTROP	V. MOLOTOV

Secret Supplementary Protocol

The undersigned Plenipotentiaries declare the agreement of the Government of the German Reich and the Government of the U.S.S.R. upon the following:

The Secret Supplementary Protocol signed on August 23, 1939 [*see Document No. 6*], shall be amended in item 1 to the effect that the territory of the Lithuanian state falls to the sphere of influence of the U.S.S.R., while on the other hand, the province of Lublin and parts of the province of Warsaw fall to the sphere of influence of Germany (cf. the map attached to the Boundary and Friendship Treaty signed today). As soon as the Government of the U.S.S.R. shall take special measures on Lithuanian territory to protect its interests, the present German-Lithuanian border, for the purpose of a natural and simple boundary delineation, shall be rectified in such a way that the Lithuanian territory situated to the southwest of the line marked on the attached map shall fall to Germany.

Further it is declared that the economic agreements now in force between Germany and Lithuania shall not be affected by the measures of the Soviet Union referred to above.

Moscow, September 28, 1939
For the Government *By authority of the*
of the German Reich: *Government of the U.S.S.R.:*
 J. RIBBENTROP   V. MOLOTOV

Secret Supplementary Protocol

The undersigned Plenipotentiaries, on concluding the German-Russian Boundary and Friendship Treaty, have declared their agreement upon the following:

Both parties will tolerate in their territories no Polish agitation which affects the territories of the other party. They will suppress in their territories all beginnings of such agitation and inform each other concerning suitable measures for this purpose.

Moscow, September 28, 1939
For the Government *By authority of the*
of the German Reich: *Government of the U.S.S.R.:*
 J. RIBBENTROP   V. MOLOTOV

DECLARATION OF THE GOVERNMENT OF THE GERMAN REICH AND THE GOVERNMENT OF THE U.S.S.R. OF SEPTEMBER 28, 1939

After the Government of the German Reich and the Government of the U.S.S.R. have, by means of the treaty signed today, definitively settled the problems arising from the collapse of the Polish state and have thereby created a sure foundation for a lasting peace in Eastern Europe, they mutually express their conviction that it would serve the true interest of all peoples to put an end to the state of war existing at present between Germany on the one side and England and France on the other. Both Governments will therefore direct their common efforts, jointly with other friendly powers if occasion arises, toward attaining this goal as soon as possible.

Should, however, the efforts of the two Governments remain fruitless, this would demonstrate the fact that England and France are responsible for the continuation of the war, whereupon, in case of the continuation of the war, the Governments of Germany and of the U.S.S.R. shall engage in mutual consultations with regard to necessary measures.

Moscow, September 28, 1939

For the Government of the German Reich:	*By authority of the Government of the U.S.S.R.:*
J. RIBBENTROP	V. MOLOTOV

— 10 —

LEAGUE OF NATIONS' EXPULSION OF THE U.S.S.R., DECEMBER 14, 1939[11]

On November 30, 1939, the U.S.S.R. invaded Finland because the latter had rejected certain aggressive demands

[11] The Council Resolution is from League of Nations, *Official Journal 1939*, p. 506; the Assembly Resolution may be found in *ibid.*, p. 540.

*that included the establishment of a Soviet military base
on Finnish soil. While Finland appealed to the League of
Nations for help, Moscow recognized a puppet Finnish
Government headed by Otto Kuusinen—who had spent
most of the time since World War I in Russian exile.
Kuusinen quickly acceded to Moscow's demands, whereupon the Soviets said no war existed and refused to discuss the matter before the League. On December 14,
accordingly, the League labeled the Soviet Union an
aggressor and expelled it from membership.*

✓   ✓   ✓

RESOLUTION Adopted by the Council of the League
of Nations, December 14, 1939

The Council,

Having taken cognisance of the resolution adopted by
the Assembly on December 14th, 1939, regarding the ap-
peal of the Finnish Government;

1. Associates itself with the condemnation by the Assembly of the action of the Union of Soviet Socialist
Republics against the Finnish State; and

2. For the reasons set forth in the resolution of the
Assembly, in virtue of Article 16, paragraph 4, of the
Covenant, finds that, by its act, the Union of Soviet So-
cialist Republics has placed itself outside the League of
Nations. It follows that the Union of Soviet Socialist Re-
publics is no longer a Member of the League.

— 11 —

HITLER'S DIRECTIVE FOR THE OCCUPATION OF DENMARK AND NORWAY, MARCH 1, 1940[12]

[12] United States, Office of United States Chief of Counsel for
Prosecution of Axis Criminality, *Nazi Conspiracy and
Aggression,* 8 vols. and 2 suppl. vols. (Government Print-
ing Office, Washington, 1946-1948), VI, 1003-1005, Doc.
No. C-174.

Shortly before 5:00 A.M. on April 9, 1940, the Danish Government received from Berlin a note saying that Germany had "indubitable evidence" of Allied plans to use Scandinavia as a military base. To "protect" the region against this danger, Germany would immediately occupy Denmark and "crush" any resistance. In reality, Nazi troops entered Denmark before the Copenhagen Government could possibly reply. The procedure was duplicated in Norway. Later the Germans justified the invasions as a countermeasure to the laying of Allied mines off the coast of Norway a few days earlier. But Nazi troops had been shipped northward to Norway long before this, and the official directive for "Operation Weser" was dated March 1, 1940.

ᛉ   ᛉ   ᛉ

The Fuehrer and Supreme Commander
of the Armed Forces

Berlin, 1 March 1940
TOP SECRET By Officer only

DIRECTIVE FOR "FALL WESERUEBUNG"

1. The development of the Situation in Scandinavia required the making of all preparations for the occupation of Denmark and Norway by a part of the German Armed Forces (*"Fall Weseruebung"*). This operation should prevent British encroachment on Scandinavia and the Baltic; further it should guarantee our ore base in Sweden and give our Navy and Air Force a wider start line against Britain. The part which the Navy and the Air Force will have to play, within the limits of their capabilities, is to protect the operation against the interference of British naval and air striking forces.

In view of our military and political power in comparison with that of the Scandinavian States, the force to be employed in the "Fall Weseruebung" will be kept as small as possible. The numerical weakness will be balanced by daring actions and surprise execution. On principle, we will do our utmost to make the operation appear as a *peaceful* occupation, the object of which is the military protection of the neutrality of the Scandinavian States. Corresponding demands will be transmitted to the Governments at the beginning of the occupation. If necessary, demonstrations by the Navy and Air Force, will provide the necessary emphasis. If, in spite of this, resistance should be met with, all military means will be used to crush it.

2. I put in charge of the preparations and the conduct of the operation against Denmark and Norway the Commanding General of the XXI Army Corps, General d. I. [*der Infanterie*—of the Infantry] v. Falkenhorst (Commander of "Group XXI").

In questions of the conduct of operations the above-named is directly under my orders. The Staff is to be completed from all the three branches of the Armed Forces.

The force which will be selected for the purpose of "Fall Weseruebung" will be under separate command. They will not be allocated for other operational theatres.

The part of the Air Force detailed for the purpose of the "Weseruebung" will be tactically under the orders of Group XXI. After the completion of their task they revert to the command of Ob. d. L. [Commander-in-Chief of the Air Force].

The employment of the forces which are under direct Naval and Air Force command will take place in agreement with the Commander of Group XXI.

The administration and supply of the forces posted to Group XXI will be ensured by the branches of the Armed Forces themselves according to the demands of the Commander.

3. The crossing of the Danish border and the landings in Norway must take place *simultaneously*. I emphasize that the operations must be prepared as quickly as possible. In case the enemy seizes the initiative against Norway, we must be able to apply immediately our own countermeasures.

It is most important that the Scandinavian States as well as the Western opponents should be *taken by surprise* by our measures. All preparations, particularly those of transport and of readiness, drafting and embarkation of the troops, must be made with this factor in mind.

In case the preparations for embarkation can no longer be kept secret, the leaders and the troops will be deceived with fictitious objectives. The troops may be acquainted with the actual objectives only after putting to sea.

4. *Occupation of Denmark ("Weseruebung Sued")*

Added to this, having secured the most important places, the Group will break through as quickly as possible from Fuenen to Skagen and to the east coast. In Seeland bases will be captured early on. These will serve as starting points for later occupation. *The Navy* will provide forces for the securing of the connection Nyborg-Korsoer and for swift capture of the Kleine-Belt-Bridges as well as for landing of troops should the necessity arise. It will also prepare the defense of the coast.

The Air Force will provide squadrons, the primary object of which will be demonstrations and dropping of leaflets. Full use of the existing Danish ground defenses and air defense must be ensured.

5. *Occupation of Norway ("Weseruebung Nord")*

The task of the Group XXI: Capture by surprise of the most important places on the coast by sea and airborne operations.

The Navy will take over the preparation and carrying out of the transport by sea of the landing troops as well as the transport of the forces which will have to be brought to Oslo in a later stage of the operation. It will escort supplies and reserves on the way over by sea.

Preparations must be made for speedy completion of coastal defence in Norway.

The Air Force, after the occupation has been completed, will ensure air defence and will make use of Norwegian bases for air warfare against Britain.

6. Group XXI will make regular reports to the OKW concerning the state of preparations and will submit a chronological summary of the progress of preparations. The shortest necessary space of time between the issue of the order for "Weseruebung" and its execution must be reported.

Intended Battle Headquarters will be reported.

Code names: *Wesertag*—the day of the operation. *Weserzeit*—"H" hour.

(Signed) A. HITLER

A BRITISH OFFER OF ANGLO-FRENCH UNION, JUNE 16, 1940[13]

After little more than a month of Blitzkrieg (lightning war), the Germans held about one-fourth of France, and several French Cabinet members advocated surrender. Premier Paul Reynaud wished to continue the fight if he could get substantial support, particularly air support, from Great Britain. But after the disasters culminating in the evacuation of Dunkirk, the British Isles themselves were vulnerable to invasion and unable to help anyone else. In a desperate effort to afford psychological comfort, Great Britain, through the Cabinet, on June 16, 1940, offered to enter a constitutional union with France.[14]

At this most fateful moment in the history of the modern world the Governments of the United Kingdom and the French Republic make this declaration of indissoluble union and unyielding resolution in their common defence of justice and freedom, against subjection to a system which reduces mankind to a life of robots and slaves.

The two Governments declare that France and Great Britain shall no longer be two nations but one Franco-British Union. The constitution of the Union will provide for joint organs of defence, foreign, financial, and economic policies. Every citizen of France will enjoy immediately citizenship of Great Britain, every British subject will become a citizen of France.

---

[13] Great Britain, Parliament, *Parliamentary Debates*, Fifth Series, Volume 365. *House of Commons Official Report, Eleventh Volume of Session 1939-40*, (London, His Majesty's Stationery Office, 1940), columns 701-702.
[14] See also W. S. Churchill, *The Second World War*, 6 vols. (Boston, 1948-1953), II (*Their Finest Hour*), 208-209.

Both countries will share responsibility for the repair of the devastation of war, wherever it occurs in their territories, and the resources of both shall be equally, and as one, applied to that purpose.

During the war there shall be a single war Cabinet, and all the forces of Britain and France, whether on land, sea, or in the air, will be placed under its direction. It will govern from wherever it best can. The two Parliaments will be formally associated.

The nations of the British Empire are already forming new armies. France will keep her available forces in the field, on the sea, and in the air.

The Union appeals to the United States to fortify the economic resources of the Allies and to bring her powerful material aid to the common cause.

The Union will concentrate its whole energy against the power of the enemy no matter where the battle may be. And thus we shall conquer.

— 13 —

THE FRANCO-GERMAN ARMISTICE, JUNE 25, 1940[15]

After France requested an armistice, Chancellor Adolf Hitler conferred with Premier Benito Mussolini regarding prospective terms. Then, on June 21, 1940, the Germans received a French armistice delegation in the Compiègne Forest in the same railway coach to which the German armistice delegation of 1919 had been summoned.

[15] *The New York Times*, June 26, 1940. Reprinted by permission. Another translation may be found in United States, Department of State, Publication No. 6312, *Documents on German Foreign Policy 1918-1945* (Government Printing Office, Washington, 1956), Series D, IX, 671-676.

*Following acceptance of the German terms, the French-
men flew to Italy and accepted Rome's demands. The
armistice became effective and firing ceased in the early
morning of June 25, 1940. The British Fleet, by prompt
action, largely nullified the naval clauses of the armistice.*

✓   ✓   ✓

ARMISTICE AGREEMENT BETWEEN THE GERMAN HIGH
COMMAND OF THE ARMED FORCES AND FRENCH
PLENIPOTENTIARIES, COMPIÈGNE, JUNE 22, 1940

Between the chief of the High Command of the armed
forces, Col. Gen. [Wilhelm] Keitel, commissioned by the
Fuehrer of the German Reich and Supreme Commander
in Chief of the German Armed Forces, and the fully authorized plenipotentiaries of the French Government, General [Charles L. C.] Huntziger, chairman of the delegation; Ambassador [Léon] Noel, Rear Admiral [Maurice
R.] LeLuc, Army Corps General [Georges] Parisot and
Air Force General [Jean-Marie Joseph] Bergeret, the
following armistice treaty was agreed upon:

ARTICLE I. The French Government directs a cessation of fighting against the German Reich in France as
well as in French possessions, colonies, protectorate territories, mandates as well as on the seas.

It [the French Government] directs the immediate laying down of arms of French units already encircled by
German troops.

ARTICLE II. To safeguard the interests of the German Reich, French State territory north and west of the
line drawn on the attached map will be occupied by German troops.

As far as the parts to be occupied still are not in control of German troops, this occupation will be carried out
immediately after the conclusion of this treaty.

ARTICLE III. In the occupied parts of France the
German Reich exercises all rights of an occupying power.
The French Government obligates itself to support with
every means the regulations resulting from the exercise
of these rights and to carry them out with the aid of
French administration.

All French authorities and officials of the occupied territory, therefore, are to be promptly informed by the

French Government to comply with the regulations of the German military commanders and to cooperate with them in a correct manner.

It is the intention of the German Government to limit the occupation of the west coast after ending hostilities with England to the extent absolutely necessary.

The French Government is permitted to select the seat of its government in unoccupied territory, or, if it wishes, to move to Paris. In this case, the German Government guarantees the French Government and its central authorities every necessary alleviation so that they will be in a position to conduct the administration of unoccupied territory from Paris.

ARTICLE IV. French armed forces on land, on the sea, and in the air are to be demobilized and disarmed in a period still to be set. Excepted are only those units which are necessary for maintenance of domestic order. Germany and Italy will fix their strength. The French armed forces in the territory to be occupied by Germany are to be hastily withdrawn into territory not to be occupied and be discharged. These troops, before marching out, shall lay down their weapons and equipment at the places where they are stationed at the time this treaty becomes effective. They are responsible for orderly delivery to German troops.

ARTICLE V. As a guarantee for the observance of the armistice, the surrender, undamaged, of all those guns, tanks, tank defense weapons, war planes, anti-aircraft artillery, infantry weapons, means of conveyance, and munitions can be demanded from the units of the French armed forces which are standing in battle against Germany and which at the time this agreement goes into force are in territory not to be occupied by Germany.

The German armistice commission will decide the extent of delivery.

ARTICLE VI. Weapons, munitions, and war apparatus of every kind remaining in the unoccupied portion of France are to be stored and/or secured under German and/or Italian control—so far as not released for the arming allowed to French units.

The German High Command reserves the right to direct all those measures which are necessary to exclude unauthorized use of this material. Building of new war apparatus in unoccupied territory is to be stopped immediately.

ARTICLE VII. In occupied territory, all the land and coastal fortifications, with weapons, munitions, and apparatus and plants of every kind are to be surrendered undamaged. Plans of these fortifications, as well as plans of those already conquered by German troops, are to be handed over.

Exact plans regarding prepared blastings, land mines, obstructions, time fuses, barriers for fighting, etc., shall be given to the German High Command. These hindrances are to be removed by French forces upon German demand.

ARTICLE VIII. The French war fleet is to collect in ports to be designated more particularly, and under German and/or Italian control to demobilize and lay up—with the exception of those units released to the French Government for protection of French interests in its colonial empire.

The peacetime stations of ships should control the designation of ports.

The German Government solemnly declares to the French Government that it does not intend to use the French War Fleet which is in harbors under German control for its purposes in war, with the exception of units necessary for the purposes of guarding the coast and sweeping mines.

It further solemnly and expressly declares that it does not intend to bring up any demands respecting the French War Fleet at the conclusion of a peace.

All warships outside France are to be recalled to France with the exception of that portion of the French War Fleet which shall be designated to represent French interests in the colonial empire.

ARTICLE IX. The French High Command must give the German High Command the exact location of all mines which France has set out, as well as information on the other harbor and coastal obstructions and defense facilities. Insofar as the German High Command may require, French forces must clear away the mines.

ARTICLE X. The French Government is obligated to forbid any portion of its remaining armed forces to undertake hostilities against Germany in any manner.

The French Government also will prevent members of

its armed forces from leaving the country and prevent armaments of any sort, including ships, planes, etc., being taken to England or any other place abroad.

The French Government will forbid French citizens to fight against Germany in the service of States with which the German Reich is still at war. French citizens who violate this provision are to be treated by German troops as insurgents.

ARTICLE XI. French commercial vessels of all sorts, including coastal and harbor vessels which are now in French hands, may not leave port until further notice. Resumption of commercial voyages will require approval of the German and Italian Governments.

French commercial vessels will be recalled by the French Government or, if return is impossible, the French Government will instruct them to enter neutral harbors.

All confiscated German commercial vessels are, on demand, to be returned [to Germany] undamaged.

ARTICLE XII. Flight by any airplane over French territory shall be prohibited. Every plane making a flight without German approval will be regarded as an enemy by the German Air Force and treated accordingly.

In unoccupied territory, air fields and ground facilities of the air force shall be under German and Italian control.

Demand may be made that such air fields be rendered unusable. The French Government is required to take charge of all foreign airplanes in the unoccupied region to prevent flights. They are to be turned over to the German armed forces.

ARTICLE XIII. The French Government obligates itself to turn over to German troops in the occupied region all facilities and properties of the French armed forces in undamaged condition.

It [the French Government] also will see to it that harbors, industrial facilities, and docks are preserved in their present condition and damaged in no way.

The same stipulations apply to transportation routes and equipment, especially railways, roads, and canals, and to the whole communications network and equipment, waterways and coastal transportation services.

Additionally, the French Government is required on demand of the German High Command to perform all necessary restoration labor on these facilities.

The French Government will see to it that in the occupied region necessary technical personnel and rolling stock of the railways and other transportation equipment, to a degree normal in peacetime, be retained in service.

ARTICLE XIV. There is an immediate prohibition of transmission for all wireless stations on French soil. Resumption of wireless connections from the unoccupied portion of France requires a special regulation.

ARTICLE XV. The French Government obligates itself to convey transit freight between the German Reich and Italy through unoccupied territory to the extent demanded by the German Government.

ARTICLE XVI. The French Government, in agreement with the responsible German officials, will carry out the return of population into occupied territory.

ARTICLE XVII. The French Government obligates itself to prevent every transference of economic valuables and provisions from the territory to be occupied by German troops into unoccupied territory or abroad.

These valuables and provisions in occupied territory are to be disposed of only in agreement with the German Government. In that connection, the German Government will consider the necessities of life of the population in unoccupied territory.

ARTICLE XVIII. The French Government will bear the costs of maintenance of German occupation troops on French soil.

ARTICLE XIX. All German war and civil prisoners in French custody, including those under arrest and convicted who were seized and sentenced because of acts in favor of the German Reich, shall be surrendered immediately to German troops.

The French Government is obliged to surrender upon demand all Germans named by the German Government in France as well as in French possessions, colonies, protectorate territories, and mandates.

The French Government binds itself to prevent removal of German war and civil prisoners from France into French possessions or into foreign countries. Regarding prisoners already taken outside of France, as well as sick and wounded German prisoners who cannot be transported, exact lists with the places of residence are to be produced. The German High Command assumes care of sick and wounded German war prisoners.

ARTICLE XX. French troops in German prison camps will remain prisoners of war until conclusion of a peace.

ARTICLE XXI. The French Government assumes responsibility for the security of all objects and valuables whose undamaged surrender or holding in readiness for German disposal is demanded in this agreement or whose removal outside the country is forbidden. The French Government is bound to compensate for all destruction, damage or removal contrary to agreement.

ARTICLE XXII. The Armistice Commission, acting in accordance with the direction of the German High Command, will regulate and supervise the carrying out of the armistice agreement. It is the task of the Armistice Commission further to insure the necessary conformity of this agreement with the Italian-French armistice.

The French Government will send a delegation to the seat of the German Armistice Commission to represent the French wishes and to receive regulations from the German Armistice Commission for executing [the agreement].

ARTICLE XXIII. This armistice agreement becomes effective as soon as the French Government also has reached an agreement with the Italian Government regarding cessation of hostilities.

Hostilities will be stopped six hours after the moment at which the Italian Government has notified the German Government of conclusion of its agreement. The German Government will notify the French Government of this time by wireless.

ARTICLE XXIV. This agreement is valid until conclusion of a peace treaty. The German Government may terminate this agreement at any time with immediate effect if the French Government fails to fulfill the obligations it assumes under the agreement.

This armistice agreement, signed in the Forest of Compiègne, June 22, 1940, at 6:50 p.m., German summer time.

HUNTZIGER
KEITEL

APPENDIX

The line mentioned in Article II of the armistice agreement begins in the east on the French-Swiss border at Geneva and runs thence nearly over the villages of Dôle,

Paray, Le Monial, and Bourges to approximately twenty kilometers east of Tours. From there it goes at a distance of twenty kilometers east of the Tours-Angoulême-Liborune railway line and extends through Mont de Marsan and Orthez to the Spanish border.

— 14 —

ESTABLISHMENT OF THE VICHY DICTATORSHIP, JULY 10, 1940[16]

Meeting at Vichy in unoccupied France, the two houses of Parliament sitting as the National Assembly on July 10, 1940, bestowed on Marshal Henri P. Pétain power to draw up a new constitution—for eventual submission to vote of the people. In no hurry to prepare and submit such a charter, Pétain simply issued a series of consecutively numbered "Constitutional Acts." Beginning with the first such act on July 11, 1940, which abolished the French presidency, the successive decrees gradually abolished the entire parliamentary system and by August, 1942, had substituted a Vichy dictatorship for the Third Republic. Two sample acts will illustrate the procedure.

[16] Constitutional Act No. 2 is from France, *Journal Officiel de la République française,* 1940, No. 168; Constitutional Act No. 7 is from France, *Journal Officiel de l'Etat français,* 1941, No. 28; the translations are reprinted with permission of the Carnegie Endowment for International Peace, Division of International Law, from R. Lemkin, *Axis Rule in Occupied Europe. Laws of Occupation. Analysis of Government. Proposals for Redress* (Washington, 1944), pp. 406-407.

Constitutional Act No. 2, Defining the authority of the Chief of the French State, July 11, 1940

We, Marshal of France, Chief of the French State, in consideration of the Constitutional Law of July 10, 1940, Decree:

ARTICLE I. *Section 1.* The Chief of the French State shall have full governmental powers. He shall appoint and revoke the appointment of ministers and of state secretaries, who shall be responsible only to him.

Section 2. He shall exercise legislative power in the Council of Ministers:

1. Until the formation of the new Assemblies.

2. After this formation, in case of tension in foreign affairs, or of a serious internal crisis, on his own decision and in the same form. In the same circumstances, he may issue all regulations of a budgetary or fiscal nature.

Section 3. He shall promulgate laws and assure their execution.

Section 4. He shall make appointments to all civil and military posts for which the law does not provide any other method of appointment.

Section 5. He shall have full power over the armed forces.

Section 6. He shall have the right of granting pardon and amnesty.

Section 7. Envoys and ambassadors of foreign countries shall be accredited to him.

He shall negotiate and ratify treaties.

Section 8. He may declare a state of siege in one or more parts of the territories.

Section 9. He may not declare war without the previous consent of the Legislative Assemblies.

ARTICLE II. All provisions of the constitutional laws of February 24, 1875, and July 16, 1875, which are incompatible with this act are hereby abrogated.

Vichy, July 11, 1940

PH. PÉTAIN

CONSTITUTIONAL ACT No. 7, JANUARY 27, 1941

We, Marshal of France, Chief of the French State, in consideration of the constitutional law of July 10, 1940, Decree:

ARTICLE 1. The state secretaries, high dignitaries, and high officials of the state shall take oath before the Chief of the State. They shall swear allegiance to his person and engage themselves to perform their duties for the welfare of the state in accordance with rules of honor and of probity.

ARTICLE 2. The state secretaries, high dignitaries, and high officials of the state shall be personally responsible to the Chief of State. This responsibility shall apply to their person and their property.

ARTICLE 3. In case any one of the above-mentioned group should prove unfaithful to his obligations, the Chief of State, after instituting an inquiry by means of a procedure upon which he shall decide, may require payment of reparation and fines, and may temporarily or definitively apply the following penalties: loss of political rights; surveillance of residence in France or in the Colonies; administrative internment; detention in a fortress.

ARTICLE 4. The imposition of penalties by virtue of the preceding article shall not prevent the prosecution, under normal judicial procedure, of crimes or offenses which may have been committed by the same persons.

ARTICLE 5. Articles 3 and 4 of the present act shall apply to former ministers, high dignitaries, and high officials who have exercised their duties within the past ten years.

Vichy, January 27, 1941

PH. PÉTAIN

— 15 —

AUTHORITY OF NAZI AMBASSADOR TO VICHY FRANCE, AUGUST 3, 1940[17]

One of the ablest German agents in prewar France, who helped to bring about its downfall, was Otto Abetz. Following the armistice, he was appointed German Ambassador to Vichy. His authority and functions were defined in a letter of August 3, 1940, from Foreign Minister Joachim von Ribbentrop to the High Command of the German Armed Forces.

✢   ✢   ✢

Ministry of Foreign Affairs, 3 August 1940

In answer to a question of the Quartermaster General, addressed to the High Command of the Armed Forces and transmitted by the latter to the Ministry of Foreign Affairs, the Führer has appointed Abetz, until now Minister, as Ambassador, and on my report has decreed the following:

I. Ambassador Abetz has the following functions in France:

   1. To advise the military agencies on political matters.

   2. To maintain permanent contact with the Vichy Government and its representatives in the occupied zone.

   3. To influence the important political personalities in the occupied zone and in the unoccupied zone in a way favorable to our intentions.

[17] *Trial of the Major War Criminals before the International Military Tribunal, Nuremberg, 14 November 1945–1 October 1946,* 42 vols. (Nuremberg, 1948), VI, 560-561 (Doc. RF-1061). The text in German may be found in *ibid.,* XXXII, 432-433 (Doc. 3614-PS).

4. To guide from the political point of view the press, the radio, and the propaganda in the occupied zone and to influence the responsive elements engaged in the molding of public opinion in the unoccupied zone.

5. To take care of the German, French, and Belgian citizens returning from internment camps.

6. To advise the secret military police and the Gestapo on the seizure of politically important documents.

7. To seize and secure all public art treasures and private art treasures, and particularly art treasures belonging to Jews, on the basis of special instructions relating thereto.

II. The Führer has expressly ordered that only Ambassador Abetz shall be responsible for all political questions in Occupied and Unoccupied France. Insofar as military interests are touched by his duties, Ambassador Abetz shall act only in agreement with the Military Command in France.

III. Ambassador Abetz will be attached to the Military Commander in France as his deputy. His domicile shall continue to be in Paris as hitherto. He will receive from me instructions for the accomplishment of his tasks and will be responsible solely to me. I shall greatly appreciate it if the High Command of the Armed Forces will give the necessary orders to the military agencies concerned as quickly as possible.

Signed: RIBBENTROP

— 16 —

HITLER ON PUNISHMENT OF OFFENDERS IN OCCUPIED TERRITORY, DECEMBER 7, 1941 [18]

In a directive which the Germans themselves labeled "Night-and-Fog Decree" (Nacht-und-Nebel Erlass), *Chancellor Adolf Hitler provided for the drastic punishment of persons committing offences against the German occupiers. In the words of General Wilhelm Keitel, who was responsible for administering the directive, Hitler was convinced that "an effective and lasting deterrence can only be achieved by capital punishment or by measures calculated to leave the relatives and the population uncertain as to the fate of the offender; transportation to Germany will serve this purpose."*

✓ ✓ ✓

The Fuehrer and Supreme Commander
of the Armed Forces

[stamp] SECRET

Directives for the prosecution of offences committed within the occupied territories against the German State or the occupying power, of December 7th, 1941.

Within the occupied territories, communistic elements and other circles hostile to Germany have increased their

[18] United States, Office of United States Chief of Counsel for Prosecution of Axis Criminality, *Nazi Conspiracy and Aggression,* 8 vols. and 2 suppl. vols. (Government Printing Office, Washington, 1946-1948), VII, 873-874 (Doc. No. L-90). The quotation in the introduction to this document and the entire directive in German may be found in *Trial of the Major War Criminals before the International Military Tribunal, Nuremberg, 14 November 1945– 1 October 1946,* 42 vols. (Nuremberg, 1948), XXVI, 245-249 (Doc. No. 669-PS) and XXXVII, 570-577 (Doc. No. 90-L).

efforts against the German State and the occupying power since the Russian campaign started. The amount and the danger of these machinations oblige us to take severe measures as a determent. First of all the following directives are to be applied:

I. Within the occupied territories, the adequate punishment for offences committed against the German State or the occupying power which endanger their security or state of readiness is on principle the death penalty.

II. The offences listed in paragraph I as a rule are to be dealt with in the occupied countries only if it is probable that sentence of death will be passed upon the offender, at least the principal offender, and if the trial and the execution can be completed in a very short time. Otherwise the offenders, at least the principal offenders, are to be taken to Germany.

III. Prisoners taken to Germany are subjected to military procedure only if particular military interests require this. In case German or foreign authorities inquire about such prisoners, they are to be told that they were arrested, but that the proceedings do not allow any further information.

IV. The Commanders in the occupied territories and the Court authorities within the framework of their jurisdiction, are personally responsible for the observance of this decree.

V. The Chief of the High Command of the Armed Forces determines in which occupied territories this decree is to be applied. He is authorized to explain and to issue executive orders and supplements. The Reich Minister of Justice will issue executive orders within his own jurisdiction.

ROOSEVELT ON THE UNITED STATES LANDINGS IN NORTH AFRICA, NOVEMBER 8, 1942[19]

Early in November, 1942, United States troops were landed at selected points in French North Africa and French West Africa. The objectives were to forestall similar German action, tighten the blockade of the "Axis," give added protection to Allied shipping, and establish an invasion base for southern Europe. Because of the psychological factors involved, President Franklin D. Roosevelt wrote a personal letter to Marshal Henri P. Pétain. The reply was disappointing.

Marshal Pétain:

I am sending this message to you as the Chef d'État of the United States to the Chef d'État of the Republic of France.

When your Government concluded the Armistice Convention in 1940, it was impossible for any of us to foresee the program of systematic plunder which the German Reich would inflict on the French people.

That program, implemented by blackmail and robbery, has deprived the French population of its means of subsistence, its savings; it has paralyzed French industry and transport; it has looted French factories and French farms —all for the benefit of a Nazi Reich and a Fascist Italy under whose Governments no liberty-loving nation could long exist.

As an old friend of France and the people of France, my anger and sympathy grow with every passing day when I consider the misery, the want, and the absence from their homes of the flower of French manhood. Germany has

[19] United States, Department of State, *Bulletin* (Government Printing Office, Washington, 1942), VII, 904-905.

neglected no opportunity to demoralize and degrade your great nation.

Today, with greedy eyes on that Empire which France so laboriously constructed, Germany and Italy are proposing to invade and occupy French North Africa in order that they may execute their schemes of domination and conquest over the whole of that continent.

I know you will realize that such a conquest of Africa would not stop there but would be the prelude to further attempts by Germany and Italy to threaten the conquest of large portions of the American Hemisphere, large dominations over the Near and Middle East, and a joining of hands in the Far East with those military leaders of Japan who seek to dominate the whole of the Pacific.

It is evident, of course, that an invasion and occupation of French North and West Africa would constitute for the United States and all of the American Republics the gravest kind of menace to their security—just as it would sound the death knell of the French Empire.

In the light of all the evidence of our enemy's intentions and plans, I have, therefore, decided to dispatch to North Africa powerful American armed forces to cooperate with the governing agencies of Algeria, Tunisia, and Morocco in repelling this latest act in the long litany of German and Italian international crime.

These indomitable American forces are equipped with massive and adequate weapons of modern warfare which will be available for your compatriots in North Africa in our mutual fight against the common enemy.

I am making all of this clear to the French Authorities in North Africa, and I am calling on them for their co-operation in repelling Axis threats. My clear purpose is to support and aid the French Authorities and their administrations. That is the immediate aim of these American armies.

I need not tell you that the ultimate and greater aim is the liberation of France and its Empire from the Axis yoke. In so doing we provide automatically for the security of the Americas.

I need not again affirm to you that the United States of America seeks no territories and remembers always the historic friendship and mutual aid which we have so greatly given to each other.

I send to you and, through you, to the people of France my deep hope and belief that we are all of us soon to enter into happier days.

FRANKLIN D. ROOSEVELT

President Roosevelt:

It is with stupor and sadness that I learned tonight of the aggression of your troops against North Africa.

I have read your message. You invoke pretexts which nothing justifies. You attribute to your enemies intentions which have not ever been manifested in acts. I have always declared that we would defend our Empire if it were attacked; you should know that we would defend it against any aggressor whoever he might be. You should know that I would keep my word.

In our misfortune I had, when requesting the armistice, protected our Empire, and it is you, who, acting in the name of a country to which so many memories and ties bind us, have taken such a cruel initiative.

France and her honor are at stake.

We are attacked; we shall defend ourselves; this is the order I am giving.

PHILIPPE PÉTAIN

— 18 —

"BLOOD, TOIL, TEARS AND SWEAT," MAY 13, 1940[20]

The Nazi invasion of Luxembourg, Belgium, and the Netherlands led to the resignation of Prime Minister Neville Chamberlain on May 10, 1940. His successor, Winston S. Churchill, made his first speech as Prime Minister

[20] Great Britain, *Parliamentary Debates, House of Commons,* Fifth Series, Volume 360, 1501-1502.

to the House of Commons three days later. This talk contained one of the most famous and inspiring phrases of modern times.[21]

✓   ✓   ✓

On Friday evening last I received His Majesty's Commission to form a new Administration. It was the evident wish and will of Parliament and the nation that this should be conceived on the broadest possible basis and that it should include all parties, both those who supported the late Government and also the parties of the Opposition. I have completed the most important part of this task. A War Cabinet has been formed of five Members, representing, with the Opposition Liberals, the unity of the nation. The three party Leaders have agreed to serve, either in the War Cabinet or in high executive office. The three Fighting Services have been filled. It was necessary that this should be done in one single day, on account of the extreme urgency and rigor of events. A number of other positions, key positions, were filled yesterday, and I am submitting a further list to His Majesty tonight. I hope to complete the appointment of the principal Ministers during tomorrow. The appointment of the other Ministers usually takes a little longer, but I trust that, when Parliament meets again, this part of my task will be completed, and that the Administration will be complete in all respects.

I considered it in the public interest to suggest that the House should be summoned to meet today. Mr. Speaker agreed, and took the necessary steps, in accordance with the powers conferred upon him by the Resolution of the House. At the end of the proceedings today, the Adjournment of the House will be proposed until Tuesday, 21st May, with, of course, provision for earlier meeting if need be. The business to be considered during that week will be notified to Members at the earliest opportunity. I now invite the House, by the Motion which stands in my name, to record its approval of the steps taken and to declare its confidence in the new Government.

To form an Administration of this scale and complexity is a serious undertaking in itself, but it must be remem-

---

[21] Cf. also the widely current phrase, "blood, sweat, and tears."

bered that we are in the preliminary stage of one of the greatest battles in history, that we are in action at many points in Norway and in Holland, that we have to be prepared in the Mediterranean, that the air battle is continuous and that many preparations, . . . have to be made here at home. In this crisis I hope I may be pardoned if I do not address the House at any length today. I hope that any of my friends and colleagues, or former colleagues, who are affected by the political reconstruction, will make allowance, all allowance, for any lack of ceremony with which it has been necessary to act. I would say to the House, as I said to those who have joined this Government: "I have nothing to offer but blood, toil, tears and sweat."

We have before us an ordeal of the most grievous kind. We have before us many, many long months of struggle and of suffering. You ask, what is our policy? I will say: It is to wage war, by sea, land, and air, with all our might and with all the strength that God can give us: to wage war against a monstrous tyranny, never surpassed in the dark, lamentable catalogue of human crime. That is our policy. You ask, what is our aim? I can answer in one word: It is victory, victory at all costs, victory in spite of all terror, victory, however long and hard the road may be; for without victory, there is no survival. Let that be realized; no survival for the British Empire; no survival for all that the British Empire has stood for, no survival for the urge and impulse of the ages, that mankind will move forward towards its goal. But I take up my task with buoyancy and hope. I feel sure that our cause will not be suffered to fail among men. At this time I feel entitled to claim the aid of all, and I say, "Come then, let us go forward together with our united strength."

HITLER'S EXPLANATION OF THE SOVIET INVASION, JUNE 21, 1941 [22]

On June 21, 1941, the German Ambassador to Moscow was ordered to inform the U.S.S.R. that, since the latter was "about to attack Germany from the rear," the German Armed Forces were immediately opposing "this threat with all the means at their disposal" (invasion). Chancellor Adolf Hitler's explanation of this development to Premier Benito Mussolini—who, although he was an ally, was not apprised of the move in advance—is interesting diplomatically and psychologically.

ᐟ   ᐟ   ᐟ

June 21, 1941

Duce!

I am writing this letter to you at a moment when months of anxious deliberation and continuous nerve-racking waiting are ending in the hardest decision of my life. I believe —after seeing the latest Russian situation map and after appraisal of numerous other reports—that I cannot take the responsibility for waiting longer, and above all, I believe that there is no other way of obviating this danger —unless it be further waiting, which, however, would necessarily lead to disaster in this or the next year at the latest.

The situation: England has lost this war. With the right of the drowning person, she grasps at every straw which, in her imagination, might serve as a sheet anchor. Nevertheless, some of her hopes are naturally not without a certain logic. England has thus far always conducted her wars

[22] United States, Department of State, Publication No. 3023, *Nazi-Soviet Relations 1939-1941. Documents from the Archives of the German Foreign Office* (Government Printing Office, Washington, 1948), pp. 349-353.

with help from the Continent. The destruction of France—in fact, the elimination of all west-European positions—is directing the glances of the British warmongers continually to the place from which they tried to start the war: to Soviet Russia.

Both countries, Soviet Russia and England, are equally interested in a Europe fallen into ruin, rendered prostrate by a long war. Behind these two countries stands the North American Union goading them on and watchfully waiting. Since the liquidation of Poland, there is evident in Soviet Russia a consistent trend, which, even if cleverly and cautiously, is nevertheless reverting firmly to the old Bolshevist tendency to expansion of the Soviet State. The prolongation of the war necessary for this purpose is to be achieved by tying up German forces in the East, so that—particularly in the air—the German Command can no longer vouch for a large-scale attack in the West. I declared to you only recently, Duce, that it was precisely the success of the experiment in Crete that demonstrated how necessary it is to make use of every single airplane in the much greater project against England. It may well happen that in this decisive battle we would win with a superiority of only a few squadrons. I shall not hesitate a moment to undertake such a responsibility if, aside from all other conditions, I at least possess the one certainty that I will not then suddenly be attacked or even threatened from the East. The concentration of Russian forces—I had General Jodl submit the most recent map to your Attaché here, General Maras[23]—is tremendous. Really, all available Russian forces are at our border. Moreover, since the approach of warm weather, work has been proceeding on numerous defenses. If circumstances should give me cause to employ the German air force against England, there is danger that Russia will then begin its strategy of extortion in the South and North, to which I would have to yield in silence, simply from a feeling of air inferiority. It would, above all, not then be possible for me without adequate support from an air force, to attack the Russian fortifications with the divisions stationed in the East. If I do not wish to expose myself to this danger, then perhaps the whole year of 1941 will go by without any change in the general situation. On the contrary. England will be all the less ready

[23] General Efisio Marras, Italian military attaché in Berlin.

for peace, for it will be able to pin its hopes on the Russian partner. Indeed, this hope must naturally even grow with the progress in preparedness of the Russian armed forces. And behind this is the mass delivery of war material from America which they hope to get in 1942.

Aside from this, Duce, it is not even certain whether we shall have this time, for with so gigantic a concentration of forces on both sides—for I also was compelled to place more and more armored units on the eastern border, and also to call Finland's and Rumania's attention to the danger—there is the possibility that the shooting will start spontaneously at any moment. A withdrawal on my part would, however, entail a serious loss of prestige for us. This would be particularly unpleasant in its possible effect on Japan. I have, therefore, after constantly racking my brains, finally reached the decision to cut the noose before it can be drawn tight. I believe, Duce, that I am hereby rendering probably the best possible service to our joint conduct of the war this year. For my over-all view is now as follows:

1) *France* is, as ever, not to be trusted. Absolute surety that North Africa will not suddenly desert does not exist.

2) *North Africa* itself, insofar as your colonies, Duce, are concerned, is probably out of danger until fall. I assume that the British, in their last attack, wanted to relieve Tobruk. I do not believe they will soon be in a position to repeat this.

3) *Spain* is irresolute and—I am afraid—will take sides only when the outcome of the war is decided.

4) In *Syria,* French resistance can hardly be maintained permanently either with or without our help.

5) An attack on *Egypt* before autumn is out of the question altogether. I consider it necessary, however, taking into account the whole situation, to give thought to the development of an operational unit in Tripoli itself which can, if necessary, also be launched against the West. Of course, Duce, the strictest silence must be maintained with regard to these ideas, for otherwise we cannot expect France to continue to grant permission to use its ports for the transportation of arms and munitions.

6) Whether or not *America* enters the war is a matter of indifference, inasmuch as she supports our opponent with all the power she is able to mobilize.

7) The situation in England itself is bad; the provision of food and raw materials is growing steadily more difficult. The martial spirit to make war, after all, lives only on hopes. These hopes are based solely on two assumptions: Russia and America. We have no chance of eliminating America. But it does lie in our power to exclude Russia. The elimination of Russia means, at the same time, a tremendous relief for Japan in East Asia, and thereby the possibility of a much stronger threat to American activities through Japanese intervention.

I have decided under these circumstances, as I already mentioned, to put an end to the hypocritical performance in the Kremlin. I assume, that is to say, I am convinced, that Finland, and likewise Rumania, will forthwith take part in this conflict, which will ultimately free Europe, for the future also, of a great danger. General Maras informed us that you, Duce, wish also to make available at least one corps. If you have that intention, Duce—which I naturally accept with a heart filled with gratitude—the time for carrying it out will still be sufficiently long, for in this immense theater of war the troops cannot be assembled at all points at the same time anyway. You, Duce, can give the decisive aid, however, by strengthening your forces in North Africa, also, if possible, looking from Tripoli toward the West, by proceeding further to build up a group which, though it be small at first, can march into France in case of a French violation of the treaty; and finally, by carrying the air war and, so far as it is possible, the submarine war, in intensified degree, into the Mediterranean.

So far as the security of the territories in the West is concerned, from Norway to and including France, we are strong enough there—so far as army troops are concerned —to meet any eventuality with lightning speed. So far as the air war on England is concerned, we shall, for a time remain on the defensive,—but this does not mean that we might be incapable of countering British attacks on Germany; on the contrary, we shall, if necessary, be in a position to start ruthless bombing attacks on British home territory. Our fighter defense, too, will be adequate. It consists of the best squadrons that we have.

As far as the war in the East is concerned, Duce, it will surely be difficult, but I do not entertain a second's doubt as to its great success. I hope, above all, that it will then be possible for us to secure a common food-supply base in the Ukraine for some time to come, which will furnish us such additional supplies as we may need in the future. I may state at this point, however, that, as far as we can tell now, this year's German harvest promises to be a very good one. It is conceivable that Russia will try to destroy the Rumanian oil region. We have built up a defense that will—or so I think—prevent the worst. Moreover, it is the duty of our armies to eliminate this threat as rapidly as possible.

If I waited until this moment, Duce, to send you this information, it is because the final decision itself will not be made until 7 o'clock tonight. I earnestly beg you, therefore, to refrain, above all, from making any explanation to your Ambassador at Moscow, for there is no absolute guarantee that our coded reports cannot be decoded. I, too, shall wait until the last moment to have my own Ambassador informed of the decisions reached.

The material that I now contemplate publishing gradually, is so exhaustive that the world will have more occasion to wonder at our forbearance than at our decision, except for that part of the world which opposes us on principle and for which, therefore, arguments are of no use.

Whatever may now come, Duce, our situation cannot become worse as a result of this step; it can only improve. Even if I should be obliged at the end of this year to leave 60 or 70 divisions in Russia, that is only a fraction of the forces that I am now continuually using on the eastern front. Should England nevertheless not draw any conclusions from the hard facts that present themselves, then we can, with our rear secured, apply ourselves with increased strength to the dispatching of our opponent. I can promise you, Duce, that what lies in our German power, will be done.

Any desires, suggestions, and assistance of which you, Duce, wish to inform me in the contingency before us, I would request that you either communicate to me personally or have them agreed upon directly by our military authorities.

In conclusion, let me say one more thing, Duce. Since I struggled through to this decision, I again feel spiritually free. The partnership with the Soviet Union, in spite of the complete sincerity of the efforts to bring about a final conciliation, was nevertheless often very irksome to me, for in some way or other it seemed to me to be a break with my whole origin, my concepts, and my former obligations. I am happy now to be relieved of these mental agonies.

With hearty and comradely greetings,

Your
ADOLF HITLER

— 20 —

THE "DESTROYER-BASES DEAL," SEPTEMBER 2, 1940[24]

One of Winston S. Churchill's early acts as prime minister was to write President Franklin D. Roosevelt of his country's desperate need for destroyers to cope with the German submarine menace. Not long thereafter, negotiations were started for the lease of some British possessions in the Atlantic as United States military bases. The two projects were combined into what was commonly called the "destroyer-bases deal." The arrangement was sealed by an exchange of letters on September 2, 1940, supplemented by a detailed agreement signed in London, March 27, 1941.

[24] United States Department of State, Publication No. 1726, *Executive Agreement Series 235: Leased Naval and Air Bases. Agreement and Exchange of Notes between the United States of America and Great Britain and Protocol between the United States, Great Britain, and Canada Concerning the Defense of Newfoundland. Signed March 27, 1941* (Government Printing Office, Washington, 1942), pp. 14-16.

EXCHANGE OF NOTES REGARDING UNITED STATES DESTROYERS AND NAVAL AND AIR FACILITIES FOR THE UNITED STATES IN BRITISH TRANSATLANTIC TERRITORIES

No. 1

THE MARQUESS OF LOTHIAN TO MR. CORDELL HULL

Washington, September 2, 1940

Sir,

I HAVE the honour, under instructions from His Majesty's Principal Secretary of State for Foreign Affairs, to inform you that in view of the friendly and sympathetic interest of His Majesty's Government in the United Kingdom in the national security of the United States and their desire to strengthen the ability of the United States to co-operate effectively with the other nations of the Americas in the defence of the Western Hemisphere, His Majesty's Government will secure the grant to the Government of the United States, freely and without consideration, of the lease for immediate establishment and use of Naval and Air bases and facilities for entrance thereto and the operation and protection thereof, on the Avalon Peninsula and on the Southern coast of Newfoundland, and on the East coast and on the Great Bay of Bermuda.

Furthermore, in view of the above and in view of the desire of the United States to acquire additional Air and Naval bases in the Caribbean and in British Guiana, and without endeavouring to place a monetary or commercial value upon the many tangible and intangible rights and properties involved, His Majesty's Government will make available to the United States for immediate establishment and use Naval and Air bases and facilities for entrance thereto and the operation and protection thereof, on the Eastern side of the Bahamas, the Southern coast of Jamaica, the Western coast of St. Lucia, the West coast of Trinidad in the Gulf of Paria, in the Island of Antigua, and in British Guiana within fifty miles of Georgetown, in exchange for Naval and Military equipment and material which the United States Government will transfer to His Majesty's Government.

All of the bases and facilities referred to in the preceding paragraphs will be leased to the United States for a period of ninety-nine years free from all rent and charges other than such compensation to be mutually agreed on to be paid by the United States in order to compensate the owners of private property for loss by expropriation or damage arising out of the establishment of the bases and facilities in question.

His Majesty's Government in the leases to be agreed upon will grant to the United States for the period of the leases all the rights, power, and authority within the bases leased, and within the limits of the territorial waters and air spaces adjacent to, or in the vicinity of, such bases, necessary to provide access to, and defence of, such bases and appropriate provisions for their control.

Without prejudice to the above-mentioned rights of the United States authorities and their jurisdiction within the leased areas, the adjustment and reconciliation between the jurisdiction of the authorities of the United States within these areas and the jurisdiction of the authorities of the territories in which these areas are situated shall be determined by common agreement.

The exact location and bounds of the aforesaid bases, the necessary seaward, coast, and anti-aircraft defenses, the location of sufficient military garrisons, stores and other necessary auxiliary facilities shall be determined by common agreement.

His Majesty's Government are prepared to designate immediately experts to meet with experts of the United States for these purposes. Should these experts be unable to agree in any particular situation except in the case of Newfoundland and Bermuda, the matter shall be settled by the Secretary of State of the United States and His Majesty's Secretary of State for Foreign Affairs.

I have, etc.

LOTHIAN

No. 2

MR. CORDELL HULL TO THE MARQUESS OF LOTHIAN

Washington, September 2, 1940

Excellency,

I HAVE received your note of 2nd September, 1940, of which the text is as follows:—

[As in NO. 1.] [25]

I am directed by the President to reply to your note as follows:

"The Government of the United States appreciates the declarations and the generous action of His Majesty's Government, as contained in your communications, which are destined to enhance the national security of the United States and greatly to strengthen its ability to co-operate effectively with the other nations of the Americas in the defence of the Western Hemisphere. It therefore gladly accepts the proposals.

"The Government of the United States will immediately designate experts to meet with experts designated by His Majesty's Government to determine upon the exact location of the Naval and Air bases mentioned in your communication under acknowledgment.

"In consideration of the declarations above quoted, the Government of the United States will immediately transfer to His Majesty's Government fifty United States Navy Destroyers generally referred to as the twelve-hundred ton type."

Accept, etc.

CORDELL HULL

— 21 —

ROOSEVELT'S "FOUR FREEDOMS" SPEECH, JANUARY 6, 1941 [26]

[25] Brackets in original.
[26] United States, 77th Congress, 1st Session, House Document No. 1, *Address Delivered by President Roosevelt to the Congress, January 6, 1941* (Government Printing Office, Washington, 1941).

When asked about his long-term peace objectives at a press conference in mid-1940, President Franklin D. Roosevelt "somewhat casually" mentioned what appeared to him to be four basic human freedoms. Then, in his message to Congress on January 6, 1941, he declared that "we look forward to a world founded upon four essential human freedoms." The phrase, "Four Freedoms," soon came to be a popular slogan. Unhappily, the President did not list obligations to correspond to the freedoms.

✓   ✓   ✓

I ADDRESS YOU, the Members of the Seventy-seventh Congress, at a moment unprecedented in the history of the Union. I use the word "unprecedented," because at no previous time has American security been as seriously threatened from without as it is today. . . .

Every realist knows that the democratic way of life is at this moment being directly assailed in every part of the world—assailed either by arms, or by secret spreading of poisonous propaganda by those who seek to destroy unity and promote discord in nations that are still at peace.

During sixteen long months this assault has blotted out the whole pattern of democratic life in an appalling number of independent nations, great and small. The assailants are still on the march, threatening other nations, great and small. . . .

As long as the aggressor nations maintain the offensive, they—not we—will choose the time and the place and the method of their attack.

That is why the future of all the American Republics is today in serious danger.

That is why this Annual Message to the Congress is unique in our history. . . .

The need of the moment is that our actions and our policy should be devoted primarily—almost exclusively—to meeting this foreign peril. For all our domestic problems are now a part of the great emergency.

Just as our national policy in internal affairs has been based upon a decent respect for the rights and the dignity of all our fellow men within our gates, so our national policy in foreign affairs has been based on a decent respect for the rights and dignity of all nations, large and small. And the justice of morality must and will win in the end.

Our national policy is this:

First, by an impressive expression of the public will and without regard to partisanship, we are committed to all-inclusive national defense.

Second, by an impressive expression of the public will and without regard to partisanship, we are committed to full support of all those resolute peoples, everywhere, who are resisting aggression and are thereby keeping war away from our Hemisphere. By this support, we express our determination that the democratic cause shall prevail; and we strengthen the defense and the security of our own nation.

Third, by an impressive expression of the public will and without regard to partisanship, we are committed to the proposition that principles of morality and considerations for our own security will never permit us to acquiesce in a peace dictated by aggressors and sponsored by appeasers. We know that enduring peace cannot be bought at the cost of other people's freedom. . . .

In the future days, which we seek to make secure, we look forward to a world founded upon four essential human freedoms.

The first is freedom of speech and expression—everywhere in the world.

The second is freedom of every person to worship God in his own way—everywhere in the world.

The third is freedom from want—which, translated into world terms, means economic understandings which will secure to every nation a healthy peacetime life for its inhabitants—everywhere in the world.

The fourth is freedom from fear—which, translated into world terms, means a world-wide reduction of armaments to such a point and in such a thorough fashion that no nation will be in a position to commit an act of physical aggression against any neighbor—anywhere in the world.

That is no vision of a distant millennium. It is a definite basis for a kind of world attainable in our own time and generation. That kind of world is the very antithesis of the so-called new order of tyranny which the dictators seek to create with the crash of a bomb.

To that new order we oppose the greater conception—the moral order. A good society is able to face schemes of world domination and foreign revolutions alike without fear. . . .

This nation has placed its destiny in the hands and heads and hearts of its millions of free men and women; and its faith in freedom under the guidance of God. Freedom means the supremacy of human rights everywhere. Our support goes to those who struggle to gain those rights or keep them. Our strength is our unity of purpose.

To that high concept there can be no end save victory.

— 22 —

THE "LEND-LEASE ACT," MARCH 11, 1941–AUGUST 21, 1945[27]

To enable the United States to lend the enemies of the Axis Powers much more material help than they could pay for, President Franklin D. Roosevelt persuaded Congress on March 11, 1941, to pass a bill "to promote the defense of the United States" by making possible "all-out" material aid to the Allies. Then, on August 21, 1945, twelve days before the Japanese surrender, President Harry S. Truman, without warning, put a stop to lend-lease activities. The suddenness of this action created many difficulties for the Allies. The total value of lend-lease aid between the dates indicated was estimated at $48,500,000,000; reverse lend-lease to the United States was estimated at $7,800,000,000.

✓   ✓   ✓

[27] *A* is from *United States Statutes at Large* (Government Printing Office, Washington, 1941), LV, 31 ff. *B* is from United States, Department of State, *Bulletin* (Government Printing Office, Washington, 1945), XIII, 284.

A

BE IT ENACTED BY THE SENATE AND
HOUSE OF REPRESENTATIVES OF THE
UNITED STATES OF AMERICA IN CONGRESS
ASSEMBLED, That this Act may be cited as "An Act to
Promote the Defense of the United States."

Section 2. As used in this Act—

(*a*) The term "defense article" means—

(1) Any weapon, munition, aircraft, vessel, or boat;

(2) Any machinery, facility, tool, material, or supply
necessary for the manufacture, production, processing, repair, servicing, or operation of any article described in
this subsection;

(3) Any component material or part of or equipment
for any article described in this subsection;

(4) Any agricultural, industrial, or other commodity
or article for defense.

Such term "defense article" includes an article described
in this subsection: Manufactured or procured pursuant to
section 3, or to which the United States or any foreign
government has or hereafter acquires title, possession, or
control.

(*b*) The term "defense information" means any plan,
specification, design, prototype, or information pertaining
to any defense article.

Section 3. (*a*) Notwithstanding the provisions of any
other law, the President may, from time to time, when he
deems it in the interest of national defense, authorize the
Secretary of War, the Secretary of the Navy, or the
head of any other department or agency of the Government—

(1) To manufacture in arsenals, factories, and shipyards under their jurisdiction, or otherwise procure, to
the extent to which funds are made available therefor, or
contracts are authorized from time to time by the Congress, or both, any defense article for the government of
any country whose defense the President deems vital to
the defense of the United States.

(2) To sell, transfer title to, exchange, lease, lend, or
otherwise dispose of, to any such government any defense
article, but no defense article not manufactured or procured under paragraph (1) shall in any way be disposed

of under this paragraph, except after consultation with the Chief of Staff of the Army or the Chief of Naval Operations of the Navy, or both. The value of defense articles disposed of in any way under authority of this paragraph, and procured from funds heretofore appropriated, shall not exceed $1,300,000,000. The value of such defense articles shall be determined by the head of the department or agency concerned or such other department, agency or officer as shall be designated in the manner provided in the rules and regulations issued hereunder. Defense articles procured from funds hereafter appropriated to any department or agency of the Government, other than from funds authorized to be appropriated under this Act, shall not be disposed of in any way under authority of this paragraph except to the extent hereafter authorized by the Congress in the Acts appropriating such funds or otherwise.

(3) To test, inspect, prove, repair, outfit, recondition, or otherwise to place in good working order, to the extent to which funds are made available therefor, or contracts are authorized from time to time by the Congress, or both, any defense article for any such government, or to procure any or all such services by private contract.

(4) To communicate to any such government any defense information, pertaining to any defense article furnished to such government under paragraph (2) of this subsection.

(5) To release for export any defense article disposed of in any way under this subsection to any such government.

(b) The terms and conditions upon which any such foreign government receives any aid authorized under subsection (a) shall be those which the President deems satisfactory, and the benefit to the United States may be payment or repayment in kind or property, or any other direct or indirect benefit which the President deems satisfactory.

(c) After June 30, 1943, or after the passage of a concurrent resolution by the two Houses before June 30, 1943, which declares that the powers conferred by or pursuant to subsection (a) are no longer necessary to promote the defense of the United States, neither the President nor the head of any department or agency shall exercise any of the powers conferred by or pursuant to subsection (a);

except that until July 1, 1946, any of such powers may be exercised to the extent necessary to carry out a contract or agreement with such a foreign government made before July 1, 1943, or before the passage of such concurrent resolution, whichever is the earlier.

(d) Nothing in this Act shall be construed to authorize or to permit the authorization of convoying vessels by naval vessels of the United States.

(e) Nothing in this Act shall be construed to authorize or to permit the authorization of the entry of any American vessel into a combat area in violation of section 3 of the Neutrality Act of 1939.

Section 4. All contracts or agreements made for the disposition of any defense article or defense information pursuant to section 3 shall contain a clause by which the foreign government undertakes that it will not, without the consent of the President, transfer title to or possession of such defense article or defense information by gift, sale, or otherwise, or permit its use by anyone not an officer, employee, or agent of such foreign government.

Section 5. (a) The Secretary of War, the Secretary of the Navy, or the head of any other department or agency of the Government involved shall, when any such defense article or defense information is exported, immediately inform the department or agency designated by the President to administer section 6 of the Act of July 2, 1940 (54 Stat. 714), of the quantities, character, value, terms of disposition, and destination of the article and information so exported.

(b) The President from time to time, but not less frequently than once every ninety days, shall transmit to the Congress a report of operations under this Act except such information as he deems incompatible with the public interest to disclose. Reports provided for under this subsection shall be transmitted to the Secretary of the Senate or the Clerk of the House of Representatives, as the case may be, if the Senate or the House of Representatives, as the case may be, is not in session.

Section 6. (a) There is hereby authorized to be appropriated from time to time, out of any money in the Treasury not otherwise appropriated, such amounts as may be necessary to carry out the provisions and accomplish the purposes of this Act.

(*b*) All money and all property which is converted into money received under section 3 from any government shall, with the approval of the Director of the Budget, revert to the respective appropriation or appropriations out of which funds were expended with respect to the defense article or defense information for which such consideration is received, and shall be available for expenditure for the purpose for which such expended funds were appropriated by law, during the fiscal year in which such funds are received and the ensuing fiscal year; but in no event shall any funds so received be available for expenditure after June 30, 1946.

Section 7. The Secretary of War, the Secretary of the Navy, and the head of the department or agency shall in all contracts or agreements for the disposition of any defense article or defense information fully protect the rights of all citizens of the United States who have patent rights in and to any such article or information which is hereby authorized to be disposed of and the payments collected for royalties on such patents shall be paid to the owners and holders of such patents.

Section 8. The Secretaries of War and of the Navy are hereby authorized to purchase or otherwise acquire arms, ammunition, and implements of war produced within the jurisdiction of any country to which section 3 is applicable, whenever the President deems such purchase or acquisition to be necessary in the interests of the defense of the United States.

Section 9. The President may, from time to time, promulgate such rules and regulations as may be necessary and proper to carry out any of the provisions of this Act; and he may exercise any power or authority conferred on him by this Act through such department, agency, or officer as he shall direct.

Section 10. Nothing in this Act shall be construed to change existing law relating to the use of the land and naval forces of the United States, except insofar as such use relates to the manufacture, procurement, and repair of defense articles, the communication of information and other noncombatant purposes enumerated in this Act.

Section 11. If any provision of this Act or the application of such provision to any circumstance shall be held invalid, the validity of the remainder of the Act and the applicability of such provision to other circumstances shall not be affected thereby.

Approved, March 11, 1941

B

The President has directed the Foreign Economic Administrator to take steps immediately to discontinue all lend-lease operations and to notify foreign governments receiving lend-lease of this action.

The President also directs that all outstanding contracts for lend-lease be canceled, except where Allied governments are willing to agree to take them over or where it is in the interest of the United States to complete them.

The Foreign Economic Administrator furthermore is instructed to negotiate with Allied governments for possible procurement by them of lend-lease inventories now in stockpile and in process of delivery.

If the military needs lend-lease supplies for the movement of troops or for occupation purposes, the military will be responsible for procurement.

It is estimated that uncompleted contracts for non-munitions and finished goods in this country not yet transferred to lend-lease countries amount to about 2 billion dollars and that lend-lease supplies in stockpile abroad amount to between 1 and 1½ billion dollars.

— 23 —

THE ATLANTIC CHARTER,
AUGUST 14, 1941 [28]

The first meeting between President Franklin D. Roosevelt and Prime Minister Winston S. Churchill, after they

[28] United States, 77th Congress, 1st Session, House Document No. 358, *Message of President Roosevelt to the Congress, August 21, 1941, Embodying Text of the Atlantic Charter* (Government Printing Office, Washington, 1941).

had come to their respective high offices, was aboard ship off Argentia, Newfoundland, in August, 1941. Among other things, the two men reached agreement on a statement of principles soon to be famous as the Atlantic Charter. In order that Roosevelt might not have to get Senate approval for the document, it was handled as a "release" instead of a treaty. Congress was officially informed thereof on August 21. On January 1, 1942, the twenty-six powers then in the United Nations subscribed to its principles.

⚞   ⚞   ⚞

Over a week ago I held several important conferences at sea with the British Prime Minister. Because of the factor of safety to British, Canadian, and American ships, and their personnel, no prior announcement of these meetings could properly be made.

At the close, a public statement by the Prime Minister and the President was made. I quote it for the information of the Congress and for the record:

"The President of the United States and the Prime Minister, Mr. Churchill, representing His Majesty's Government in the United Kingdom, have met at sea.

"They have been accompanied by officials of their two Governments, including high-ranking officers of their military, naval, and air services.

"The whole problem of the supply of munitions of war, as provided by the Lease-Lend Act, for the armed forces of the United States, and for those countries actively engaged in resisting aggression, has been further examined.

"Lord Beaverbrook, the Minister of Supply of the British Government, has joined in these conferences. He is going to proceed to Washington to discuss further details with appropriate officials of the United States Government. These conferences will also cover the supply problems of the Soviet Union.

"The President and the Prime Minister have had several conferences. They have considered the dangers to world civilization arising from the policies of military domination by conquest upon which the Hitlerite government of Germany and other governments associated therewith have embarked, and have made clear the steps which their countries are respectively taking for their safety in the face of these dangers.

"They have agreed upon the following joint declaration:

"Joint declaration of the President of the United States of America and the Prime Minister, Mr. Churchill, representing His Majesty's Government in the United Kingdom, being met together, deem it right to make known certain common principles in the national policies of their respective countries on which they base their hopes for a better future of the world.

"First, their countries seek no aggrandizement, territorial or other;

"Second, they desire to see no territorial changes that do not accord with the freely expressed wishes of the peoples concerned;

"Third, they respect the right of all peoples to choose the form of government under which they will live; and they wish to see sovereign rights and self-government restored to those who have been forcibly deprived of them;

"Fourth, they will endeavor, with due respect for their existing obligations, to further the enjoyment by all states, great or small, victor or vanquished, of access, on equal terms, to the trade and to the raw materials of the world which are needed for their economic prosperity;

"Fifth, they desire to bring about the fullest collaboration between all nations in the economic field with the object of securing, for all, improved labor standards, economic advancement, and social security;

"Sixth, after the final destruction of the Nazi tyranny, they hope to see established a peace which will afford to all nations the means of dwelling in safety within their own boundaries, and which will afford assurance that all the men in all the lands may live out their lives in freedom from fear and want;

"Seventh, such a peace should enable all men to traverse the high seas and oceans without hindrance;

"Eighth, they believe that all of the nations of the world, for realistic as well as spiritual reasons, must come to the abandonment of the use of force. Since no future peace can be maintained if land, sea, or air armaments continue to be employed by nations which threaten, or may threaten, aggression outside of their frontiers, they believe, pending the establishment of a wider and permanent system of general security, that the disarmament of such nations is essential. They will likewise aid and encourage all other practicable measures which will lighten for peace-loving peoples the crushing burden of armaments."

FRANKLIN D. ROOSEVELT
WINSTON S. CHURCHILL

The Congress and the President having heretofore determined, through the Lend-Lease Act, on the national policy of American aid to the democracies which East and West are waging war against dictatorships, the military and naval conversations at these meetings made clear gains in furthering the effectiveness of this aid.

Furthermore, the Prime Minister and I are arranging for conferences with the Soviet Union to aid it in its defense against the attack made by the principal aggressor of the modern world—Germany.

Finally, the declaration of principles at this time presents a goal which is worth while for our type of civilization to seek. It is so clear-cut that it is difficult to oppose in any major particular without automatically admitting a willingness to accept compromise with nazi-ism; or to agree to a world peace which would give to nazi-ism domination over large numbers of conquered nations. Inevitably such a peace would be a gift to nazi-ism to take breath—armed breath—for a second war to extend the control over Europe and Asia, to the American Hemisphere itself.

It is perhaps unnecessary for me to call attention once more to the utter lack of validity of the spoken or written word of the Nazi government.

It is also unnecessary for me to point out that the declaration of principles includes, of necessity, the world need for freedom of religion and freedom of information. No society of the world organized under the announced principles could survive without these freedoms which are a part of the whole freedom for which we strive.

— 24 —

THE GERMAN-ITALIAN-JAPANESE PACT, SEPTEMBER 27, 1940[29]

While the war in Europe was in progress, Japan took the opportunity to extend her hegemony rapidly in the Far East. Despite the known opposition of the United States, Premier Prince Fumimaro Konoye announced on August 1, 1940, that his country aimed "ultimately at the construction of a new order in Great East Asia." Germany and Italy, busy with the extension of their own Lebensraum *in Europe, applauded this prospect. Accordingly, the three powers signed an alliance in Berlin on September 27, 1940.*

✓   ✓   ✓

The Governments of Germany, Italy, and Japan consider it as a condition precedent of a lasting peace, that each nation of the world be given its own proper place. They have therefore decided to stand together and to cooperate with one another in their efforts in Greater East Asia and in the regions of Europe, wherein it is their prime purpose to establish and maintain a new order of things calculated to promote the prosperity and welfare of the peoples there. Furthermore, it is the desire of the three Governments to extend this cooperation to such nations in other parts of the world as are inclined to give to their endeavors a direction similar to their own, in order that their aspirations towards world peace as the ultimate goal may thus be realized. Accordingly, the Gov-

[29] United States, Office of United States Chief of Counsel for Prosecution of Axis Criminality, *Nazi Conspiracy and Aggression*, 8 vols. and 2 suppl. vols. (Government Printing Office, Washington, 1946-1948), V, 355-357, Doc. No. 2643-PS.

ernments of Germany, Italy, and Japan have agreed as follows:

ARTICLE 1. Japan recognizes and respects the leadership of Germany and Italy in the establishment of a new order in Europe.

ARTICLE 2. Germany and Italy recognize and respect the leadership of Japan in the establishment of a new order in Greater East Asia.

ARTICLE 3. Germany, Italy, and Japan agree to cooperate in their efforts on the aforesaid basis. They further undertake to assist one another with all political, economic, and military means, if one of the three Contracting Parties is attacked by a Power at present not involved in the European war or in the Chinese-Japanese conflict.

ARTICLE 4. For the purpose of implementing the present pacts, joint technical commissions, the members of which are to be appointed by the Governments of Germany, Italy, and Japan, will meet without delay.

ARTICLE 5. Germany, Italy, and Japan affirm that the aforesaid terms do not in any way affect the political status which exists at present between each of the three Contracting Parties and Soviet Russia.

ARTICLE 6. The present Pact shall come into force immediately upon signature and shall remain in force for ten years from the date of its coming into force.

At the proper time before expiration of the said term the High Contracting Parties shall, if one of them so requests, enter into negotiations for its renewal.

In faith whereof, the undersigned, duly authorized by their Governments, have signed this pact and have hereunto apposed their seals.

Done in 3 original copies at Berlin, on the 27th day of September, 1940, in the XVIIIth year of the Fascist Era, corresponding to the 27th day of the 9th month of the 15th year of the Showa era.

THE ATTACK ON PEARL HARBOR, DECEMBER 7, 1941 [30]

While two Japanese emissaries were discussing peace proposals with Secretary of State Cordell Hull on Sunday afternoon, December 7, 1941, word reached Washington that carrier-borne Japanese airplanes and Japanese submarines had attacked, with much death and destruction, the war base and units of the United States Fleet at Pearl Harbor, Oahu, Territory of Hawaii. Because the defenders appeared to be taken wholly by surprise, the President, on December 18, 1941, appointed a Commission, headed by Justice Owen J. Roberts, "to ascertain and report the facts relating to the attack" on Hawaii. The Report was submitted on January 23, 1942. The Commander-in-Chief of the Pacific Fleet at the time of the attack was Admiral Husband E. Kimmel; the Commanding General, Hawaiian Department, was Lieutenant General Walter C. Short.

✓   ✓   ✓

CONCLUSIONS

1. Effective utilization of the military power of the Nation is essential to success in war and requires: First, the coordination of the foreign and military policies of the Nation; and, second, the coordination of the operations of the Army and Navy.

2. The Secretary of State fulfilled his obligations by keeping the War and Navy Departments in close touch

[30] United States, 77th Congress, 2d Session, Senate Document No. 159, *Report of the Commission Appointed by the President to Investigate and Report the Facts Relating to the Attack Made by Japanese Armed Forces upon Pearl Harbor in the Territory of Hawaii on December 7, 1941* (Government Printing Office, Washington, 1942), pp. 19-21.

with the international situation and fully advising them respecting the course and probable termination of negotiations with Japan.

3. The Secretary of War and the Secretary of the Navy fulfilled their obligations by conferring frequently with the Secretary of State and with each other and by keeping the Chief of Staff and the Chief of Naval Operations informed of the course of the negotiations with Japan and the significant implications thereof.

4. The Chief of Staff and the Chief of Naval Operations fulfilled their obligations by consulting and co-operating with each other, and with their superiors, respecting the joint defense of the Hawaiian coastal frontier; and each knew of, and concurred in, the warnings and orders sent by the other to the responsible commanders with respect to such defense.

5. The Chief of Staff of the Army fulfilled his command responsibility by issuing a direct order in connection with his warning of probable hostilities, in the following words: "Prior to hostile Japanese action you are directed to undertake such reconnaissance and other measures as you deem necessary."

6. The Chief of Naval Operations fulfilled his command responsibility by issuing a warning and by giving a direct order to the Commander-in-Chief, Pacific Fleet, in the following words: "This despatch is to be considered a war warning" and "Execute an appropriate defensive deployment preparatory to carrying out the tasks assigned."

7. The responsible commanders in the Hawaiian area, in fulfillment of their obligation so to do, prepared plans which, if adapted to, and used for, the existing emergency, would have been adequate.

8. In the circumstances the responsibility of these commanders was to confer upon the question of putting into effect and adapting their joint defense plans.

9. These commanders failed to confer with respect to the warnings and orders issued on and after November 27, and to adapt and use existing plans to meet the emergency.

10. The order for alert No. 1 of the Army command in Hawaii was not adequate to meet the emergency envisaged in the warning messages.

11. The state of readiness of the naval forces on the

morning of December 7 was not such as was required to meet the emergency envisaged in the warning messages.

12. Had orders issued by the Chief of Staff and the Chief of Naval Operations, November 27, 1941, been complied with, the aircraft warning system of the Army should have been operating; the distant reconnaissance of the Navy, and the inshore air patrol of the Army, should have been maintained; the anti-aircraft batteries of the Army and similar shore batteries of the Navy, as well as additional anti-aircraft artillery located on vessels of the fleet in Pearl Harbor, should have been manned and supplied with ammunition; and a high state of readiness of aircraft should have been in effect. None of these conditions was in fact inaugurated or maintained for the reason that the responsible commanders failed to consult and cooperate as to necessary action based upon the warnings and to adopt measures enjoined by the orders given them by the chiefs of the Army and Navy commands in Washington.

13. There were deficiencies in personnel, weapons, equipment, and facilities to maintain all the defenses on a war footing for extended periods of time, but these deficiencies should not have affected the decision of the responsible commanders as to the state of readiness to be prescribed.

14. The warning message of December 7, intended to reach both commanders in the field at about 7 A.M. Hawaiian time, December 7, 1941, was but an added precaution, in view of the warnings and orders previously issued. If the message had reached its destination at the time intended, it would still have been too late to be of substantial use, in view of the fact that the commanders had failed to take measures and make dispositions prior to the time of its anticipated receipt, which would have been effective to warn of the attack or to meet it.

15. The failure of the officers in the War Department to observe that General Short, neither in his reply of November 27 to the Chief of Staff's message of that date, nor otherwise, had reported the measures taken by him, and the transmission of two messages concerned chiefly with sabotage which warned him not to resort to illegal methods against sabotage or espionage, and not to take

measures which would alarm the civil population, and the failure to reply to his message of November 29 outlining in full all the actions he had taken against sabotage only, and referring to nothing else, tended to lead General Short to believe that what he had done met the requirements of the warnings and orders received by him.

16. The failure of the Commanding General, Hawaiian Department, and the Commander-in-Chief, Pacific Fleet, to confer and cooperate with respect to the meaning of the warnings received and the measures necessary to comply with the orders given them under date of November 27, 1941, resulted largely from a sense of security due to the opinion prevalent in diplomatic, military, and naval circles, and in the public press, that any immediate attack by Japan would be in the Far East. The existence of such a view, however prevalent, did not relieve the commanders of the responsibility for the security of the Pacific Fleet and our most important outpost.

17. In the light of the warnings and directions to take appropriate action, transmitted to both commanders between November 27 and December 7, and the obligation under the system of coordination then in effect for joint cooperative action on their part, it was a dereliction of duty on the part of each of them not to consult and confer with the other respecting the meaning and intent of the warnings, and the appropriate measures of defense required by the imminence of hostilities. The attitude of each, that he was not required to inform himself of, and his lack of interest in, the measures undertaken by the other to carry out the responsibility assigned to such other under the provisions of the plans then in effect, demonstrated on the part of each a lack of appreciation of the responsibilities vested in them and inherent in their positions as Commander-in-Chief, Pacific Fleet, and Commanding General, Hawaiian Department.

18. The Japanese attack was a complete surprise to the commanders, and they failed to make suitable dispositions to meet such an attack. Each failed properly to evaluate the seriousness of the situation. These errors of judgment were the effective causes for the success of the attack.

19. Causes contributory to the success of the Japanese attack were:

Disregard of international law and custom relating to declaration of war by the Japanese and the adherence by the United States to such laws and customs.

Restrictions which prevented effective counterespionage.

Emphasis in the warning messages on the probability of aggressive Japanese action in the Far East, and on anti-sabotage measures.

Failure of the War Department to reply to the message relating to the anti-sabotage measures instituted by the Commanding General, Hawaiian Department.

Nonreceipt by the interested parties, prior to the attack, of the warning message of December 7, 1941.

20. When the attack developed on the morning of December 7, 1941, the officers and enlisted men of both services were present in sufficient number and were in fit condition to perform any duty. Except for a negligible number, the use of intoxicating liquor on the preceding evening did not affect their efficiency.

21. Subordinate commanders executed their superiors' orders without question. They were not responsible for the state of readiness prescribed.

Respectfully submitted.

> OWEN J. ROBERTS
> W. H. STANDLEY
> J. M. REEVES
> FRANK R. McCOY
> JOSEPH T. McNARNEY

, — 26 —

ROOSEVELT'S WAR MESSAGE ON JAPAN, DECEMBER 8, 1941 [31]

[31] United States, Department of State, Publications No. 2008 and 2016, *Papers Relating to the Foreign Relations of the United States. Japan: 1931-1941.* 2 vols. (Government Printing Office, Washington, 1943), II, 793-794.

The Japanese declaration of war on the United States (and on Great Britain) came several hours after the attack on Pearl Harbor. On December 8, President Franklin D. Roosevelt delivered his war message to Congress. The existence of a state of war with Japan was acknowledged by a vote of 82 to 0 in the Senate, and 388 to 1 in the House.

✸   ✸   ✸

Yesterday, December 7, 1941—a date which will live in infamy—the United States of America was suddenly and deliberately attacked by naval and air forces of the Empire of Japan.

The United States was at peace with that Nation and, at the solicitation of Japan, was still in conversation with its Government and its Emperor looking toward the maintenance of peace in the Pacific. Indeed, one hour after Japanese air squadrons had commenced bombing in Oahu, the Japanese Ambassador to the United States and his colleague delivered to the Secretary of State a formal reply to a recent American message. While this reply stated that it seemed useless to continue the existing diplomatic negotiations, it contained no threat or hint of war or armed attack.

It will be recorded that the distance of Hawaii from Japan makes it obvious that the attack was deliberately planned many days or even weeks ago. During the intervening time the Japanese Government has deliberately sought to deceive the United States by false statements and expressions of hope for continued peace.

The attack yesterday on the Hawaiian Islands has caused severe damage to American naval and military forces. Very many American lives have been lost. In addition, American ships have been reported torpedoed on the high seas between San Francisco and Honolulu.

Yesterday the Japanese Government also launched an attack against Malaya.

Last night Japanese forces attacked Hong Kong.

Last night Japanese forces attacked Guam.

Last night Japanese forces attacked the Philippine Islands.

Last night the Japanese attacked Wake Island.

This morning the Japanese attacked Midway Island.

Japan has, therefore, undertaken a surprise offensive extending throughout the Pacific area. The facts of yesterday speak for themselves. The people of the United States have already formed their opinions and well understand the implications to the very life and safety of our Nation.

As Commander-in-Chief of the Army and Navy I have directed that all measures be taken for our defense.

Always will we remember the character of the onslaught against us.

No matter how long it may take us to overcome this premeditated invasion, the American people in their righteous might will win through to absolute victory.

I believe I interpret the will of the Congress and of the people when I assert that we will not only defend ourselves to the uttermost but will make very certain that this form of treachery shall never endanger us again.

Hostilities exist. There is no blinking at the fact that our people, our territory, and our interests are in grave danger.

With confidence in our armed forces—with the unbounded determination of our people—we will gain the inevitable triumph—so help us God.

I ask that the Congress declare that since the unprovoked and dastardly attack by Japan on Sunday, December 7, a state of war has existed between the United States and the Japanese Empire.

                    FRANKLIN D. ROOSEVELT

The White House, December 8, 1941

— 27 —

UNITED STATES DECLARATION OF WAR ON GERMANY, DECEMBER 11, 1941 [32]

Germany and Italy declared war on the United States on December 11, in accordance with Article 3 of their Tripartite Pact with Japan. (See Document No. 24.) Congress responded to the two challenges with identical joint resolutions of December 11, 1941. The German resolution passed in the Senate by a vote of 88 to 0, and in the House by 393 to 1. On Italy, the balloting was 90 to 0 in the Senate, and 399 to 1 in the House. Representative Jeanette Rankin of Montana voted "present" on both occasions.

✓   ✓   ✓

JOINT RESOLUTION DECLARING THAT A STATE OF WAR EXISTS BETWEEN THE GOVERNMENT OF GERMANY AND THE GOVERNMENT AND THE PEOPLE OF THE UNITED STATES AND MAKING PROVISION TO PROSECUTE THE SAME

WHEREAS the Government of Germany has formally declared war against the Government and the people of the United States of America:

Therefore be it

Resolved by the Senate and House of Representatives of the United States of America in Congress assembled, That the state of war between the United States and the Government of Germany which has thus been thrust upon the United States is hereby formally declared; and the President is hereby authorized and directed to employ the

[32] United States, Department of State, Publication No. 1983, *Peace and War. United States Foreign Policy 1931-1941* (Government Printing Office, Washington), 1943, Doc. No. 272, p. 849.

entire naval and military forces of the United States and the resources of the Government to carry on war against the Government of Germany; and, to bring the conflict to a successful termination, all of the resources of the country are hereby pledged by the Congress of the United States.

Approved, December 11, 1941, 3:05 P.M., E.S.T.

— 28 —

THE CASABLANCA CONFERENCE, JANUARY 14-24, 1943 [33]

About ten weeks after the initial landing of United States forces in French North Africa, President Franklin D. Roosevelt and Prime Minister Winston S. Churchill held their fourth wartime meeting. This conference in Morocco brought together, at least outwardly, the two leading anti-Axis, but alienated, French generals, Charles de Gaulle and Henri Giraud. It also was the setting for an announcement to the press on January 24 that the Allies would fight until the Axis Powers surrendered "unconditionally." Item A was published as a Casablanca communiqué on January 26, 1943; item B is a quotation from the notes used by President Roosevelt at the press conference.

✓   ✓   ✓

[33] *A* is from United States, Department of State, *Bulletin* (Govenment Printing Office, Washington, 1943), VIII, 93-94; *B* is from R. E. Sherwood, *Roosevelt and Hopkins. An Intimate History* (Harper & Brothers, New York, 1948), pp. 696-697. Reprinted by permission of the publishers.

A

THE CASABLANCA CONFERENCE

On January 26, 1943, at 10 P.M., EWT, the following communiqué, cabled from Casablanca, Morocco, was made public:

The President of the United States and the Prime Minister of Great Britain have been in conference near Casablanca since January 14.

They were accompanied by the combined Chiefs of Staff of the two countries:

[*Here follow the names of the civil and military officials who were at the conference.*]

For ten days the combined staffs have been in constant session, meeting two or three times a day and recording progress at intervals to the President and the Prime Minister.

The entire field of the war was surveyed theater by theater throughout the world, and all resources were marshaled for a more intense prosecution of the war by sea, land, and air.

Nothing like this prolonged discussion between two allies has ever taken place before. Complete agreement was reached between the leaders of the two countries and their respective staffs upon war plans and enterprises to be undertaken during the campaigns of 1943 against Germany, Italy, and Japan with a view to drawing the utmost advantage from the markedly favorable turn of events at the close of 1942.

Premier Stalin was cordially invited to meet the President and the Prime Minister, in which case the meeting would have been held very much farther to the east. He was unable to leave Russia at this time on account of the great offensive which he himself, as Commander-in-Chief, is directing.

The President and the Prime Minister realized up to the full the enormous weight of the war which Russia is successfully bearing along her whole land front, and their prime object has been to draw as much weight as possible off the Russian armies by engaging the enemy as heavily as possible at the first selected points.

Premier Stalin has been fully informed of the military proposals.

The President and the Prime Minister have been in communication with Generalissimo Chiang Kai-shek. They have apprised him of the measures which they are undertaking to assist him in China's magnificent and unrelaxing struggle for the common cause.

The occasion of the meeting between the President and the Prime Minister made it opportune to invite General Giraud (General Henri Honoré Giraud, High Commissioner of French Africa) to confer with the Combined Chiefs of Staff and to arrange for a meeting between him and General de Gaulle (General Charles de Gaulle, Fighting French Commander). The two generals have been in close consultation.

The President and the Prime Minister and their combined staffs, having completed their plans for the offensive campaigns of 1943, have now separated in order to put them into active and concerted execution.

B

The President and the Prime Minister, after a complete survey of the world war situation, are more than ever determined that peace can come to the world only by a total elimination of German and Japanese war power. This involves the simple formula of placing the objective of this war in terms of an unconditional surrender by Germany, Italy, and Japan. Unconditional surrender by them means a reasonable assurance of world peace, for generations. Unconditional surrender means not the destruction of the German populace, nor of the Italian or Japanese populace, but does mean the destruction of a philosophy in Germany, Italy, and Japan which is based on the conquest and subjugation of other people.

THE MOSCOW CONFERENCE OF FOREIGN MINISTERS, OCTOBER 19-30, 1943 [34]

The first of several wartime meetings of Allied foreign ministers occurred in Moscow, October 19-30, 1943. Here the foreign secretaries of the United States, Great Britain, and the U.S.S.R. drafted a number of declarations; one, on general security, also was signed by the Chinese Ambassador to Moscow. After the war, the Soviet Union acted in disregard of the Declaration on Austria.

ꜰ   ꜰ   ꜰ

ANGLO-SOVIET-AMERICAN COMMUNIQUÉ, RELEASED, NOVEMBER 1, 1943

The Conference of Foreign Secretaries of the United States of America, Mr. Cordell Hull, of the United Kingdom, Mr. Anthony Eden, and of the Soviet Union, Mr. V. M. Molotov, took place at Moscow from the 19th to 30th of October 1943. There were twelve meetings.

In addition to the Foreign Secretaries the following took part in the Conference:

[*Here follows a list of all the participants.*]

The agenda included all the questions submitted for discussion by the three Governments. Some of the questions called for final decisions and these were taken. On other questions, after discussion, decisions of principle were taken: these questions were referred for detailed consideration to commissions specially set up for the purpose or reserved for treatment through diplomatic channels. Other questions again were disposed of by an exchange of views.

---

[34] United States, Department of State, *Bulletin* (Government Printing Office, Washington, 1943), IX, 307-311.

The Governments of the United States, the United Kingdom, and the Soviet Union have been in close cooperation in all matters concerning the common war effort. But this is the first time that the Foreign Secretaries of the three Governments have been able to meet together in conference.

In the first place there were frank and exhaustive discussions of measures to be taken to shorten the war against Germany and her satellites in Europe. Advantage was taken of the presence of military advisers, representing the respective Chiefs of Staff, in order to discuss definite military operations, with regard to which decisions had been taken and which are already being prepared, and in order to create a basis for the closest military cooperation in the future between the three countries.

Second only to the importance of hastening the end of the war was the unanimous recognition by the three Governments that it was essential in their own national interests and in the interest of all peace-loving nations to continue the present close collaboration and cooperation in the conduct of the war into the period following the end of hostilities, and that only in this way could peace be maintained and the political, economic, and social welfare of their peoples fully promoted.

This conviction is expressed in a declaration in which the Chinese Government joined during the Conference and which was signed by the three Foreign Secretaries and the Chinese Ambassador at Moscow on behalf of their governments. This declaration, published today, provides for even closer collaboration in the prosecution of the war and in all matters pertaining to the surrender and disarmament of the enemies with which the four countries are respectively at war. It sets forth the principles upon which the four Governments agree that a broad system of international cooperation and security should be based. Provision is made for the inclusion of all other peace-loving nations, great and small, in the system.

The Conference agreed to set up machinery for ensuring the closest cooperation between the three Governments in the examination of European questions arising as the war develops. For this purpose the Conference decided to establish in London a European Advisory Commission to study these questions and to make joint recommendations to the three Governments.[35]

Provision was made for continuing, when necessary, tripartite consultations of representatives of the three Governments in the respective capitals through the existing diplomatic channels.

The Conference also agreed to establish an Advisory Council for matters relating to Italy, to be composed in the first instance of representatives of their three Governments and of the French Committee of National Liberation. Provision is made for addition to this Council of representatives of Greece and Yugoslavia in view of their special interests arising out of the aggressions of Fascist Italy upon their territory during the present war. This Council will deal with day-to-day questions, other than military operations, and will make recommendations designed to coordinate Allied policy with regard to Italy.

The three Foreign Secretaries considered it appropriate to reaffirm, by a declaration published today, the attitude of their Governments in favor of the restoration of democracy in Italy.

The three Foreign Secretaries declared it to be the purpose of their Governments to restore the independence of Austria. At the same time, they reminded Austria that in the final settlement account will be taken of efforts that Austria may make towards its own liberation. The declaration on Austria is published today.

The Foreign Secretaries issued at the Conference a declaration by President Roosevelt, Prime Minister Churchill, and Premier Stalin containing a solemn warning that at the time of granting any armistice to any German Government those German officers and men and members of the Nazi Party who have had any connection with atrocities and executions in countries overrun by German forces will be taken back to the countries in which their abominable crimes were committed to be charged and punished according to the laws of those countries.

In the atmosphere of mutual confidence and understand-

---

[35] This Commission admitted a French delegate in November, 1944. The Potsdam Conference of July-August, 1945 replaced the Commission by a Council of Foreign Ministers. (*See Document No. 33.*)

ing which characterized all the work of the Conference, consideration was also given to other important questions. These included not only questions of a current nature, but also questions concerning treatment of Hitlerite Germany and its satellites, economic cooperation, and the assurance of general peace.

DECLARATION OF FOUR NATIONS ON GENERAL SECURITY

The Governments of the United States of America, the United Kingdom, the Soviet Union, and China:

united in their determination, in accordance with the Declaration by the United Nations of January 1, 1942, and subsequent declarations, to continue hostilities against those Axis powers with which they respectively are at war until such powers have laid down their arms on the basis of unconditional surrender;

conscious of their responsibility to secure the liberation of themselves and the peoples allied with them from the menace of aggression;

recognizing the necessity of ensuring a rapid and orderly transition from war to peace and of establishing and maintaining international peace and security with the least diversion of the world's human and economic resources for armaments;

jointly declare:

1. That their united action, pledged for the prosecution of the war against their respective enemies, will be continued for the organization and maintenance of peace and security.

2. That those of them at war with a common enemy will act together in all matters relating to the surrender and disarmament of that enemy.

3. That they will take all measures deemed by them to be necessary to provide against any violation of the terms imposed upon the enemy.

4. That they recognize the necessity of establishing at the earliest practicable date a general international organization, based on the principle of the sovereign equality of all peace-loving states, and open to membership by all such states, large and small, for the maintenance of international peace and security.

5. That for the purpose of maintaining international

peace and security pending the re-establishment of law and order and the inauguration of a system of general security, they will consult with one another and, as occasion requires, with other members of the United Nations with a view to joint action on behalf of the community of nations.

6. That after the termination of hostilities they will not employ their military forces within the territories of other states except for the purposes envisaged in this declaration and after joint consultation.

7. That they will confer and cooperate with one another and with other members of the United Nations to bring about a practicable general agreement with respect to the regulation of armaments in the postwar period.

V. MOLOTOV, ANTHONY EDEN, CORDELL HULL, FOO PING-SHEUNG

Moscow, 30th October, 1943

DECLARATION REGARDING ITALY

The Foreign Secretaries of the United States, the United Kingdom, and the Soviet Union have established that their three Governments are in complete agreement that Allied policy towards Italy must be based upon the fundamental principle that Fascism and all its evil influences and emanations shall be utterly destroyed and that the Italian people shall be given every opportunity to establish governmental and other institutions based upon democratic principles.

The Foreign Secretaries of the United States of America and the United Kingdom declare that the action of their Governments from the inception of the invasion of Italian territory, in so far as paramount military requirements have permitted, has been based upon this policy.

In the furtherance of this policy in the future the Foreign Secretaries of the three Governments are agreed that the following measures are important and should be put into effect:

1. It is essential that the Italian Government should be made more democratic by the introduction of representatives of those sections of the Italian people who have always opposed Fascism.

2. Freedom of speech, of religious worship, of political belief, of the press, and of public meeting shall be restored

in full measure to the Italian people, who shall also be entitled to form anti-Fascist political groups.

3. All institutions and organizations created by the Fascist regime shall be suppressed.

4. All Fascist or pro-Fascist elements shall be removed from the administration and from the institutions and organizations of a public character.

5. All political prisoners of the Fascist regime shall be released and accorded full amnesty.

6. Democratic organs of local government shall be created.

7. Fascist chiefs and other persons known or suspected to be war criminals shall be arrested and handed over to justice.

In making this declaration the three Foreign Secretaries recognize that so long as active military operations continue in Italy the time at which it is possible to give full effect to the principles set out above will be determined by the Commander-in-Chief on the basis of instructions received through the Combined Chiefs of Staff. The three Governments, parties to this declaration, will, at the request of any one of them, consult on this matter.

It is further understood that nothing in this resolution is to operate against the right of the Italian people ultimately to choose their own form of government.

DECLARATION ON AUSTRIA

The Governments of the United Kingdom, the Soviet Union, and the United States of America are agreed that Austria, the first free country to fall a victim to Hitlerite aggression, shall be liberated from German domination.

They regard the annexation imposed upon Austria by Germany on March 15, 1938, as null and void. They consider themselves as in no way bound by any changes effected in Austria since that date. They declare that they wish to see re-established a free and independent Austria, and thereby to open the way for the Austrian people themselves, as well as those neighboring states which will be faced with similar problems, to find that political and economic security which is the only basis for lasting peace.

Austria is reminded, however, that she has a responsibility which she cannot evade for participation in the war on the side of Hitlerite Germany, and that in the final settlement, account will inevitably be taken of her own contribution to her liberation.

DECLARATION ON GERMAN ATROCITIES

The United Kingdom, the United States, and the Soviet Union have received from many quarters evidence of atrocities, massacres, and cold-blooded mass executions which are being perpetrated by the Hitlerite forces in the many countries they have overrun and from which they are now being steadily expelled. The brutalities of Hitlerite domination are no new thing and all the peoples or territories in their grip have suffered from the worst form of government by terror. What is new is that many of these territories are now being redeemed by the advancing armies of the liberating Powers and that in their desperation, the recoiling Hitlerite Huns are redoubling their ruthless cruelties. This is now evidenced with particular clearness by monstrous crimes of the Hitlerites on the territory of the Soviet Union which is being liberated from the Hitlerites, and on French and Italian territory.

Accordingly, the aforesaid three allied Powers, speaking in the interests of the thirty-three United Nations, hereby solemnly declare and give full warning of their declaration as follows:

At the time of the granting of any armistice to any government which may be set up in Germany, those German officers and men and members of the Nazi Party who have been responsible for, or have taken a consenting part in, the above atrocities, massacres, and executions will be sent back to the countries in which their abominable deeds were done in order that they may be judged and punished according to the laws of these liberated countries and of the free governments which will be created therein. Lists will be compiled in all possible detail from all these countries, having regard especially to invaded parts of the Soviet Union, to Poland and Czechoslovakia, to Yugoslavia and Greece, including Crete and other islands, to Norway, Denmark, the Netherlands, Belgium, Luxemburg, France, and Italy.

Thus, the Germans who take part in wholesale shootings of Italian officers or in the execution of French, Dutch, Belgian, or Norwegian hostages or of Cretan peasants, or who have shared in the slaughters inflicted on the people of Poland or in territories of the Soviet Union which are now being swept clear of the enemy, will know that they will be brought back to the scene of their crimes and judged on the spot by the peoples whom they have outraged. Let those who have hitherto not imbrued their hands with innocent blood beware lest they join the ranks of the guilty, for most assuredly the three allied Powers will pursue them to the uttermost ends of the earth and will deliver them to their accusers in order that justice may be done.

The above declaration is without prejudice to the case of the major criminals, whose offenses have no particular geographical localization and who will be punished by the joint decision of the Governments of the Allies.

ROOSEVELT, CHURCHILL, STALIN

— 30 —

THE FIRST CAIRO CONFERENCE, NOVEMBER 22-26, 1943 [36]

En route to a meeting with Premier Joseph Stalin, the Messrs. Franklin D. Roosevelt and Winston S. Churchill stopped off at Cairo, Egypt, for a talk with President Chiang Kai-shek of China. Since the Soviet Union was still at peace with Japan, no representative was present from Moscow. The participants agreed that after victory they would deprive Japan of all colonial conquests and give eventual independence to Korea.

✓   ✓   ✓

[36] United States, Department of State, *Bulletin* (Government Printing Office, Washington, 1943), IX, 393.

Joint Communiqué, Cairo, Egypt,
Released, December 1, 1943

The several military missions have agreed upon future military operations against Japan. The three great allies expressed their resolve to bring unrelenting pressure against their brutal enemies by sea, land, and air. This pressure is already rising.

The three great allies are fighting this war to restrain and punish the aggression of Japan. They covet no gain for themselves and have no thought of territorial expansion. It is their purpose that Japan shall be stripped of all the islands in the Pacific which she has seized or occupied since the beginning of the First World War in 1914, and that all the territories Japan has stolen from the Chinese, such as Manchuria, Formosa, and the Pescadores, shall be restored to the Republic of China. Japan will also be expelled from all other territories which she has taken by violence and greed. The aforesaid three great powers, mindful of the enslavement of the people of Korea, are determined that in due course Korea shall become free and independent.

With these objects in view the three allies, in harmony with those of the United Nations at war with Japan, will continue to persevere in the serious and prolonged operations necessary to procure the unconditional surrender of Japan.

— 31 —

THE TEHRAN CONFERENCE,
DECEMBER 1, 1943 [37]

[37] *A* is from United States, Department of State, *Bulletin* (Government Printing Office, Washington, 1943), IX, 409-410; *B* is from *The New York Times*, March 25, 1947, reprinted by permission.

In complete disregard of the fact that for the first twenty-two months of the war it had not helped Great Britain and France by opening a "second front" against Germany—had, indeed, continued to supply the Nazis with much-needed goods—the Soviet Union, after being invaded by the Germans, became tremendously impatient with, and suspicious of, the delay in the opening of a second front by the Western Allies. In part to allay Soviet suspicions that the West would be happy to see the Nazis and Bolsheviks destroy each other, and in part to forestall a separate Nazi-Soviet peace, Franklin D. Roosevelt and Winston S. Churchill agreed to meet Premier Joseph Stalin in Tehran, Iran. The declarations under A were made public in December 1943; the agreement under B remained secret until March, 1947. The Declaration on Iran also was signed by Shah Mohammed Riza Pahlevi.

✓   ✓   ✓

A

Declaration of the Three Powers

We—The President of the United States, the Prime Minister of Great Britain, and the Premier of the Soviet Union, have met these four days past, in this, the capital of our ally, Iran, and have shaped and confirmed our common policy.

We express our determination that our nations shall work together in war and in the peace that will follow.

As to war—our military staffs have joined in our round-table discussions, and we have concerted our plans for the destruction of the German forces. We have reached complete agreement as to the scope and timing of the operations to be undertaken from the east, west, and south.

The common understanding which we have here reached guarantees that victory will be ours.

And as to peace—we are sure that our concord will win an enduring peace. We recognize fully the supreme responsibility resting upon us and all the United Nations to make a peace which will command the goodwill of the overwhelming mass of the peoples of the world and banish the scourge and terror of war for many generations.

With our diplomatic advisors we have surveyed the problems of the future. We shall seek the cooperation and active participation of all nations, large and small, whose peoples in heart and mind are dedicated, as are our own peoples, to the elimination of tyranny and slavery, oppression and intolerance. We will welcome them, as they may choose to come, into a world family of democratic nations.

No power on earth can prevent our destroying the German armies by land, their U Boats by sea, and their war plants from the air.

Our attack will be relentless and increasing.

Emerging from these cordial conferences, we look with confidence to the day when all people of the world may live free lives, untouched by tyranny, and according to their varying desires and their own consciences.

We came here with hope and determination. We leave here, friends in fact, in spirit, and in purpose.

ROOSEVELT, CHURCHILL, AND STALIN

Signed at Tehran, December 1, 1943

DECLARATION REGARDING IRAN

The President of the United States of America, the Premier of the Union of Soviet Socialist Republics, and the Prime Minister of the United Kingdom, having consulted with each other and with the Prime Minister of Iran, desire to declare the mutual agreement of their three Governments regarding their relations with Iran.

The Governments of the United States of America, the Union of Soviet Socialist Republics, and the United Kingdom recognize the assistance which Iran has given in the prosecution of the war against the common enemy, particularly by facilitating transportation of supplies from overseas to the Soviet Union. The three Governments realize that the war has caused special economic difficulties for Iran, and they are agreed that they will continue to make available to the Government of Iran such economic assistance as may be possible, having regard to the heavy demands made upon them by their world-wide military operations and to the world-wide shortage of transport, raw materials, and supplies for civilian consumption.

With respect to the postwar period, the Governments of the United States of America, the Union of Soviet Socialist Republics, and the United Kingdom are in accord with the Government of Iran that any economic problem confronting Iran at the close of hostilities should receive full consideration along with those of the other members of the United Nations by conferences or international agencies held or created to deal with international economic matters.

The Governments of the United States of America, the Union of Soviet Socialist Republics, and the United Kingdom are at one with the Government of Iran in their desire for the maintenance of the independence, sovereignty, and territorial integrity of Iran. They count upon the participation of Iran together with all other peace-loving nations in the establishment of international peace, security, and prosperity after the war in accordance with the principles of the Atlantic Charter, to which all four Governments have continued to subscribe.

B

AGREEMENT ON THE MILITARY PLANS FOR THE DEFEAT OF GERMANY, TEHRAN, IRAN, DECEMBER 1, 1943

The Conference:

(1) Agreed that the Partisans in Yugoslavia should be supported by supplies and equipment to the greatest possible extent, and also by commando operations;

(2) Agreed that, from the military point of view, it was most desirable that Turkey should come into the war on the side of the Allies before the end of the year;

(3) Took note of Marshal Stalin's statement that if Turkey found herself at war with Germany, and as a result Bulgaria declared war on Turkey or attacked her, the Soviet would immediately be at war with Bulgaria. The Conference further took note that this fact could be explicitly stated in the forthcoming negotiations to bring Turkey into the war;

(4) Took note that Operation OVERLORD [the landings in Normandy] would be launched during May, 1944, in conjunction with an operation against Southern France. The latter operation would be undertaken in as great a strength as availability of landing craft permitted. The conference further took note of Marshal Stalin's statement that the Soviet forces would launch an offensive at about the same time with the object of preventing the

German forces from transferring from the Eastern to the Western Front;

(5) Agreed that the military staffs of the Three Powers should henceforward keep in close touch with each other in regard to the impending operations in Europe. In particular it was agreed that a cover plan to mystify and mislead the enemy as regards these operations should be concerted between the staffs concerned.

(*Signed*);

FRANKLIN D. ROOSEVELT, JOSEPH V. STALIN, WINSTON S. CHURCHILL

— 32 —

THE YALTA CONFERENCE, FEBRUARY 4-11, 1945 [38]

President Franklin D. Roosevelt, Prime Minister Winston S. Churchill, and Premier Joseph Stalin met for the last time at Yalta in the Crimea from February 4-11, 1945. The protocol of the proceedings was released in March 1947, at which time the Council of Foreign Ministers (see Document No. 33) was discussing treaty terms for Austria and Germany at a meeting in Moscow. The complete text of the "Yalta Papers" was released by the Department of State on March 17, 1955.

DEPARTMENT OF STATE

For the press   March 24, 1947
                                                No. 239

[38] United States, Department of State, *Press Release No. 239*, March 24, 1947.

PROTOCOL OF THE PROCEEDINGS OF THE CRIMEA CONFERENCE

The Crimea Conference of the Heads of the Governments of the United States of America, the United Kingdom, and the Union of Soviet Socialist Republics, which took place from February 4th to 11th, came to the following conclusions:

I. WORLD ORGANISATION

It was decided:

(1) that a United Nations Conference on the proposed world organisation should be summoned for Wednesday, 25th April, 1945, and should be held in the United States of America.

(2) the Nations to be invited to this Conference should be:

(*a*) the United Nations as they existed on the 8th February, 1945; and

(*b*) such of the Associated Nations as have declared war on the common enemy by 1st March, 1945. (For this purpose by the term "Associated Nations" was meant the eight Associated Nations and Turkey.) When the Conference on World Organisation is held, the delegates of the United Kingdom and United States of America will support a proposal to admit to original membership two Soviet Socialist Republics, i.e., the Ukraine and White Russia.

(3) that the United States Government on behalf of the Three Powers should consult the Government of China and the French Provisional Government in regard to decisions taken at the present Conference concerning the proposed World Organisation.

(4) that the text of the invitation to be issued to all the nations which would take part in the United Nations Conference should be as follows:

INVITATION

"The Government of the United States of America, on behalf of itself and of the Governments of the United Kingdom, the Union of Soviet Socialist Republics, and the Republic of China, and of the Provisional Government of the French Republic, invite the Government of ————

to send representatives to a Conference of the United Nations to be held on 25th April, 1945, or soon thereafter, at San Francisco in the United States of America to prepare a Charter for a General International Organisation for the maintenance of international peace and security.

"The above-named governments suggest that the Conference consider as affording a basis for such a Charter the Proposals for the Establishment of a General International Organization, which were made public last October as a result of the Dumbarton Oaks Conference, and which have now been supplemented by the following provisions for Section C of Chapter VI:

"C. VOTING

"'1. Each member of the Security Council should have one vote.

"'2. Decisions of the Security Council on procedural matters should be made by an affirmative vote of seven members.

"'3. Decisions of the Security Council on all other matters should be made by an affirmative vote of seven members including the concurring votes of the permanent members; provided that, in decisions under Chapter VIII, Section C, a party to a dispute should abstain from voting.'

"Further information as to arrangements will be transmitted subsequently.

"In the event that the Government of ———— desires in advance of the Conference to present views or comments concerning the proposals, the Government of the United States of America will be pleased to transmit such views and comments to the other participating Governments."

TERRITORIAL TRUSTEESHIP

It was agreed that the five Nations which will have permanent seats on the Security Council should consult each other prior to the United Nations Conference on the question of territorial trusteeship.

The acceptance of this recommendation is subject to its being made clear that territorial trusteeship will only apply to (*a*) existing mandates of the League of Nations; (*b*) territories detached from the enemy as a result of the present war; (c) any other territory which might voluntarily be placed under trusteeship; and (d) no discussion of actual territories is contemplated at the forthcoming United Nations Conference or in the preliminary consultations, and it will be a matter for subsequent agreement which territories within the above categories will be placed under trusteeship.

II. Declaration on Liberated Europe

The following declaration has been approved:

"The Premier of the Union of Soviet Socialist Republics, the Prime Minister of the United Kingdom, and the President of the United States of America have consulted with each other in the common interests of the peoples of their countries and those of liberated Europe. They jointly declare their mutual agreement to concert during the temporary period of instability in liberated Europe the policies of their three governments in assisting the peoples of the former Axis satellite states of Europe to solve by democratic means their pressing political and economic problems.

"The establishment of order in Europe and the rebuilding of national economic life must be achieved by processes which will enable the liberated peoples to destroy the last vestiges of Nazism and Fascism and to create democratic institutions of their own choice. This is a principle of the Atlantic Charter—the right of all peoples to choose the form of government under which they will live—the restoration of sovereign rights and self-government to those peoples who have been forcibly deprived of them by the aggressor nations.

"To foster the conditions in which the liberated peoples may exercise these rights, the three governments will jointly assist the people in any European liberated state or former Axis satellite state in Europe where in their judgment conditions require (a) to establish conditions of internal peace; (b) to carry out emergency measures for the relief of distressed peoples; (c) to form interim governmental authorities broadly representative of all democratic elements in the population and pledged to the earliest possible establishment through free elections of governments responsive to the will of the people; and (d) to facilitate where necessary the holding of such elections.

"The three governments will consult the other United Nations and provisional authorities or other governments in Europe when matters of direct interest to them are under consideration.

"When, in the opinion of the three governments, conditions in any European liberated state or any former Axis satellite state in Europe make such action necessary, they will immediately consult together on the measures necessary to discharge the joint responsibilities set forth in this declaration.

"By this declaration we reaffirm our faith in the principles of the Atlantic Charter, our pledge in the Declaration by the United Nations, and our determination to build in cooperation with other peace-loving nations world order under law, dedicated to peace, security, freedom and general well-being of all mankind.

"In issuing this declaration the Three Powers express the hope that the Provisional Government of the French Republic may be associated with them in the procedure suggested."

III. DISMEMBERMENT OF GERMANY

It was agreed that Article 12 (*a*) of the Surrender Terms for Germany should be amended to read as follows:

"The United Kingdom, the United States of America, and the Union of Soviet Socialist Republics shall possess supreme authority with respect to Germany. In the exercise of such authority they will take such steps, including the complete disarmament, demilitarization, and dismemberment of Germany as they deem requisite for future peace and security."

The study of the procedure for the dismemberment of Germany was referred to a committee, consisting of Mr. Eden (Chairman), Mr. Winant, and Mr. Gousev. This body would consider the desirability of associating with it a French representative.

IV. ZONE OF OCCUPATION FOR THE FRENCH AND CONTROL COUNCIL FOR GERMANY

It was agreed that a zone in Germany, to be occupied by the French Forces, should be allocated to France. This zone would be formed out of the British and American zones and its extent would be settled by the British and

Americans in consultation with the French Provisional Government.

It was also agreed that the French Provisional Government should be invited to become a member of the Allied Control Council for Germany.

V. REPARATION

The following protocol has been approved:

PROTOCOL

ON THE TALKS BETWEEN THE HEADS OF THE THREE GOVERNMENTS AT THE CRIMEAN CONFERENCE ON THE QUESTION OF THE GERMAN REPARATION IN KIND

1. Germany must pay in kind for the losses caused by her to the Allied nations in the course of the war. Reparations are to be received in the first instance by those countries which have borne the main burden of the war, have suffered the heaviest losses, and have organised victory over the enemy.

2. Reparation in kind is to be exacted from Germany in three following forms:

(*a*) Removals within two years from the surrender of Germany or the cessation of organised resistance from the national wealth of Germany located on the territory of Germany herself, as well as outside herself, as well as outside her territory (equipment, machine tools, ships, rolling stock, German investments abroad, shares of industrial, transport, and other enterprises in Germany, etc.), these removals to be carried out chiefly for purpose of destroying the war potential of Germany.

(*b*) Annual deliveries of goods from current production for a period to be fixed.

(*c*) Use of German labour.

3. For the working out on the above principles of a detailed plan for exaction of reparation from Germany an Allied Reparation Commission will be set up in Moscow. It will consist of three representatives—one from the Union of Soviet Socialist Republics, one from the United Kingdom, and one from the United States of America.

4. With regard to the fixing of the total sum of the reparation, as well as the distribution of it among the countries which suffered from the German aggression, the

Soviet and American delegations agreed as follows:

"The Moscow Reparation Commission should take in its initial studies as a basis for discussion the suggestion of the Soviet Government that the total sum of the reparation in accordance with the points (*a*) and (*b*) of the paragraph 2 should be 20 billion dollars and that 50 per cent of it should go to the Union of Soviet Socialist Republics."

The British delegation was of the opinion that pending consideration of the reparation question by the Moscow Reparation Commission no figures of reparation should be mentioned.

The above Soviet-American proposal has been passed to the Moscow Reparation Commission as one of the proposals to be considered by the Commission.

VI. Major War Criminals

The Conference agreed that the question of the major war criminals should be the subject of enquiry by the three Foreign Secretaries for report in due course after the close of the Conference.

VII. Poland

The following Declaration on Poland was agreed by the Conference:

"A new situation has been created in Poland as a result of her complete liberation by the Red Army. This calls for the establishment of a Polish Provisional Government which can be more broadly based than was possible before the recent liberation of the Western part of Poland. The Provisional Government which is now functioning in Poland should therefore be reorganized on a broader democratic basis with the inclusion of democratic leaders from Poland itself and from Poles abroad. This new Government should then be called the Polish Provisional Government of National Unity.

"M. Molotov, Mr. Harriman, and Sir A. Clark Kerr are authorised as a commission to consult in the first instance in Moscow with members of the present Provisional Government and with other Polish democratic leaders from within Poland and from abroad, with a view to the reorganisation of the present Government along the above lines. This Polish Provisional Government of National

Unity shall be pledged to the holding of free and unfettered elections as soon as possible on the basis of universal suffrage and secret ballot. In these elections all democratic and anti-Nazi parties shall have the right to take part and to put forward candidates.

"When a Polish Provisional Government of National Unity has been properly formed in conformity with the above, the Government of the U.S.S.R., which now maintains diplomatic relations with the present Provisional Government of Poland, and the Government of the United Kingdom and the Government of the United States of America will establish diplomatic relations with the new Polish Provisional Government of National Unity, and will exchange ambassadors by whose reports the respective Governments will be kept informed about the situation in Poland.

"The three Heads of Government consider that the Eastern frontier of Poland should follow the Curzon Line with digressions from it in some regions of five to eight kilometres in favour of Poland. They recognise that Poland must receive substantial accessions of territory in the North and West. They feel that the opinion of the new Polish Provisional Government of National Unity should be sought in due course on the extent of these accessions and that the final delimitation of the Western frontier of Poland should thereafter await the peace conference."

VIII. YUGOSLAVIA

It was agreed to recommend to Marshal Tito and to Dr. Subasic:

(a) that the Tito-Subasic Agreement should immediately be put into effect and a new Government formed on the basis of the Agreement.

(b) that as soon as the new Government has been formed it should declare:

(i) that the Anti-Fascist Assembly of National Liberation (AUNOJ) will be extended to include members of the last Yugoslav Skupstina who have not compromised themselves by collaboration with the enemy, thus forming a body to be known as a temporary Parliament and

(ii) that legislative acts passed by the Anti-Fascist Assembly of National Liberation (AUNOJ) will be subject to subsequent ratification by a Constituent Assembly; and that this statement should be published in the Communiqué of the Conference.

IX. ITALO-YUGOSLAV FRONTIER
ITALO-AUSTRIAN FRONTIER

Notes on these subjects were put in by the British delegation, and the American and Soviet delegations agreed to consider them and give their views later.

X. YUGOSLAV-BULGARIAN RELATIONS

There was an exchange of views between the Foreign Secretaries on the question of the desirability of a Yugoslav-Bulgarian pact of alliance. The question at issue was whether a state still under an armistice regime could be allowed to enter into a treaty with another state. Mr. Eden suggested that the Bulgarian and Yugoslav Governments should be informed that this could not be approved. Mr. Stettinius suggested that the British and American Ambassadors should discuss the matter further with M. Molotov in Moscow. M. Molotov agreed with the proposal of Mr. Stettinius.

XI. SOUTHEASTERN EUROPE

The British Delegation put in notes for the consideration of the colleagues on the following subjects:

(*a*) The Control Commission in Bulgaria.

(*b*) Greek claims upon Bulgaria, more particularly with reference to reparations.

(*c*) Oil equipment in Rumania.

XII. IRAN

Mr. Eden, Mr. Stettinius, and M. Molotov exchanged views on the situation in Iran. It was agreed that this matter should be pursued through the diplomatic channel.

XIII. MEETINGS OF THE THREE FOREIGN SECRETARIES

The Conference agreed that permanent machinery should be set up for consultation between the three Foreign Secretaries; they should meet as often as necessary, probably about every three or four months.

These meetings will be held in rotation in the three capitals, the first meeting being held in London.

XIV. The Montreux Convention and the Straits

It was agreed that at the next meeting of the three Foreign Secretaries to be held in London, they should consider proposals which it was understood the Soviet Government would put forward in relation to the Montreux Convention and report to their Governments. The Turkish Government should be informed at the appropriate moment.

The foregoing Protocol was approved and signed by the three Foreign Secretaries at the Crimean Conference, February 11, 1945.

E. R. STETTINIUS, JR.; M. MOLOTOV; ANTHONY EDEN

AGREEMENT REGARDING JAPAN

The leaders of the three Great Powers—the Soviet Union, the United States of America, and Great Britain—have agreed that in two or three months after Germany has surrendered and the war in Europe has terminated, the Soviet Union shall enter into the war against Japan on the side of the Allies on condition that:

1. The status quo in Outer Mongolia (The Mongolian People's Republic) shall be preserved;

2. The former rights of Russia violated by the treacherous attack of Japan in 1904 shall be restored, viz.:

(a) the southern part of Sakhalin, as well as all the islands adjacent to it, shall be returned to the Soviet Union,

(b) the commercial port of Dairen shall be internationalized, the pre-eminent interests of the Soviet Union in this port being safeguarded and the lease of Port Arthur as a naval base of the U.S.S.R. restored,

(c) the Chinese-Eastern Railroad and the South-Manchurian Railroad which provides an outlet to Dairen shall be jointly operated by the establishment of a joint Soviet-Chinese Company, it being understood that the pre-eminent interests of the Soviet Union shall be safeguarded and that China shall retain full sovereignty in Manchuria;

3. The Kuril islands shall be handed over to the Soviet Union.

It is understood, that the agreement concerning Outer

Mongolia and the ports and railroads referred to above will require concurrence of Generalissimo Chiang Kai-shek. The President will take measures in order to obtain this concurrence on advice from Marshal Stalin.

The Heads of the three Great Powers have agreed that these claims of the Soviet Union shall be unquestionably fulfilled after Japan has been defeated.

For its part the Soviet Union expresses its readiness to conclude with the National Government of China a pact of friendship and alliance between the U.S.S.R. and China in order to render assistance to China with its armed forces for the purpose of liberating China from the Japanese yoke.

JOSEPH V. STALIN; FRANKLIN D. ROOSEVELT; WINSTON S. CHURCHILL

February 11, 1945

— 33 —

THE POTSDAM (BERLIN) CONFERENCE, JULY 17– AUGUST 2, 1945 [39]

Following the surrender of Germany in May, 1945 (see Document No. 38) *and the intensification of the struggle against Japan, another top-level conference was held, this time at Potsdam, near Berlin. The veteran leaders present were Premier Joseph Stalin and President Chiang Kai-shek; the United States and Great Britain were represented by newcomers. Harry S. Truman had become President upon the death of his predecessor on April 12, 1945. Laborite leader Clement R. Attlee had be-*

[39] United States, Department of State, *Press Release No. 238,* March 24, 1947.

*come British Prime Minister after the defeat of his pred-
ecessor at the polls on July 15, 1945. This conference replaced the former European Advisory Commission* (see
Document No. 29) *by a Council of Foreign Ministers
representing the four powers mentioned above and France.*

✶   ✶   ✶

Berlin, August 1, 1945

There is attached hereto the agreed protocol of the
Berlin Conference.

JOSEPH V. STALIN; HARRY TRUMAN; C. R. ATTLEE

Protocol of the Proceedings of the Berlin Conference

The Berlin Conference of the three Heads of Government of the U.S.S.R., U.S.A., and U.K., which took place
from July 17 to August 2, 1945, came to the following conclusions:

I. Establishment of a Council of Foreign Ministers

A. The Conference reached the following agreement for
the establishment of a Council of Foreign Ministers to do
the necessary preparatory work for the peace settlements:

"(1) There shall be established a Council composed of
the Foreign Ministers of the United Kingdom, the Union
of Soviet Socialist Republics, China, France, and the
United States.

"(2) (i) The Council shall normally meet in London
which shall be the permanent seat of the joint Secretariat
which the Council will form. Each of the Foreign Ministers will be accompanied by a high-ranking Deputy, duly
authorized to carry on the work of the Council in the absence of his Foreign Minister, and by a small staff of technical advisers.

"(ii) The first meeting of the Council shall be held in
London not later than September 1st, 1945. Meetings may
be held by common agreement in other capitals as may be
agreed from time to time.

"(3) (i) As its immediate important task, the Council
shall be authorized to draw up, with a view to their submission to the United Nations, treaties of peace with Italy,

Rumania, Bulgaria, Hungary, and Finland, and to propose settlements of territorial questions outstanding on the termination of the war in Europe. The Council shall be utilized for the preparation of a peace settlement for Germany to be accepted by the Government of Germany when a government adequate for the purpose is established.

"(ii) For the discharge of each of these tasks the Council will be composed of the Members representing those States which were signatory to the terms of surrender imposed upon the enemy State concerned. For the purposes of the peace settlement for Italy, France shall be regarded as a signatory to the terms of surrender for Italy. Other Members will be invited to participate when matters directly concerning them are under discussion.

"(iii) Other matters may from time to time be referred to the Council by agreement between the Member Governments.

"(4) (i) Whenever the Council is considering a question of direct interest to a State not represented thereon, such State should be invited to send representatives to participate in the discussion and study of that question.

"(ii) The Council may adapt its procedure to the particular problems under consideration. In some cases it may hold its own preliminary discussions prior to the participation of other interested States. In other cases, the Council may convoke a formal conference of the States chiefly interested in seeking a solution of the particular problem."

B. It was agreed that the three Governments should each address an identical invitation to the Governments of China and France to adopt this text and to join in establishing the Council. The text of the approved invitation was as follows:

Council of Foreign Ministers: Draft for identical invitation to be sent separately by each of the Three Governments to the Governments of China and France

"The Governments of the United Kingdom, the United States, and the U.S.S.R. consider it necessary to begin without delay the essential preparatory work upon the peace settlements in Europe. To this end they are agreed that there should be established a Council of the Foreign Ministers of the Five Great Powers to prepare treaties of peace with the European enemy States for submission to the United Nations. The Council would also be empowered to propose settlements of outstanding territorial questions in Europe and to consider such other matters as member Governments might agree to refer to it.

"The text adopted by the Three Governments is as follows:

(Here insert final agreed text of the Proposal as quoted above.)

"In agreement with the Governments of the *United States and USSR, His Majesty's Government in the United Kingdom and USSR, the United States Government, the United Kingdom, and the Soviet Government* extend a cordial invitation to the Government of China (France) to adopt the text quoted above and to join in setting up the Council. *His Majesty's Government, the United States Government, the Soviet Government,* attach much importance to the participation of the *Chinese Government (French Government)* in the proposed arrangements and they hope to receive an early and favorable reply to this invitation."

C. It was understood that the establishment of the Council of Foreign Ministers for the specific purposes named in the text would be without prejudice to the agreement of the Crimea Conference that there should be periodical consultation between the Foreign Secretaries of the United States, the Union of Soviet Socialist Republics, and the United Kingdom.

D. The Conference also considered the position of the European Advisory Commission in the light of the Agreement to establish the Council of Foreign Ministers. It was noted with satisfaction that the Commission had ably discharged its principal tasks by the recommendations that it had furnished for the terms of surrender for Germany, for the zones of occupation in Germany and Austria, and for the inter-Allied control machinery in these countries. It was felt that further work of a detailed character for the coordination of Allied policy for the control of Germany and Austria would in future fall within the competence of the Control Council at Berlin and the Allied Commission at Vienna. Accordingly, it was agreed to recommend that the European Advisory Commission be dissolved.

II. The Principles to Govern the Treatment of Germany in the Initial Control Period

A. *Political Principles*

1. In accordance with the Agreement on Control Machinery in Germany, supreme authority in Germany is exercised, on instructions from their respective Governments, by the Commanders-in-Chief of the armed forces of the United States of America, the United Kingdom, the Union of Soviet Socialist Republics, and the French Republic, each in his own zone of occupation, and also jointly, in matters affecting Germany as a whole, in their capacity as members of the Control Council.

2. So far as is practicable, there shall be uniformity of treatment of the German population throughout Germany.

3. The purposes of the occupation of Germany by which the Control Council shall be guided are:

(i) The complete disarmament and demilitarization of Germany and the elimination or control of all German industry that could be used for military production.

To these ends:

(*a*) All German land, naval, and air forces, the S. S., S. A., S. D., and Gestapo,[40] with all their organizations, staffs, and institutions, including the General Staff, the Officers' Corps, Reserve Corps, military schools, war veterans' organizations and all other military and semi-military organizations, together with all clubs and associations which serve to keep alive the military tradition in Germany, shall be completely and finally abolished in such manner as permanently to prevent the revival or reorganization of German militarism and Nazism;

(*b*) All arms, ammunition, and implements of war and all specialized facilities for their production shall be held at the disposal of the Allies or destroyed. The maintenance and production of all aircraft and all arms, ammunition, and implements of war shall be prevented.

(ii) To convince the German people that they have suffered a total military defeat and that they cannot escape

---

[40] S. S. for *Schutzstaffeln or* "Elite Guards"; S. A. for *Sturmabteilungen* or storm troops; S. D. for *Sicherheitsdienst* or intelligence; and Gestapo for *Geheime Staats-Polizei* or secret police.

responsibility for what they have brought upon themselves, since their own ruthless warfare and the fanatical Nazi resistance have destroyed German economy and made chaos and suffering inevitable.

(iii) To destroy the National Socialist Party and its affiliated and supervised organizations, to dissolve all Nazi institutions, to ensure that they are not revived in any form, and to prevent all Nazi and militarist activity or propaganda.

(iv) To prepare for the eventual reconstruction of German political life on a democratic basis and for eventual peaceful cooperation in international life by Germany.

4. All Nazi laws which provided the basis of the Hitler regime or established discriminations on grounds of race, creed, or political opinion shall be abolished. No such discriminations, whether legal, administrative, or otherwise, shall be tolerated.

5. War criminals and those who have participated in planning or carrying out Nazi enterprises involving or resulting in atrocities of war crimes shall be arrested and brought to judgment. Nazi leaders, influential Nazi supporters, and high officials of Nazi organizations and institutions and any other persons dangerous to the occupation or its objectives shall be arrested and interned.

6. All members of the Nazi Party who have been more than nominal participants in its activities and all other persons hostile to Allied purposes shall be replaced by persons who, by their political and moral qualities, are deemed capable of assisting in developing genuine democratic institutions in Germany.

7. German education shall be so controlled as completely to eliminate Nazi and militarist doctrines and to make possible the successful development of democratic ideas.

8. The judicial system will be reorganized in accordance with the principles of democracy, of justice under law, and of equal rights for all citizens without distinction of race, nationality, or religion.

9. The administration in Germany should be directed towards the decentralization of the political structure and the development of local responsibility. To this end:

(i) local self-government shall be restored throughout Germany on democratic principles and in particular through elective councils as rapidly as is consistent with military security and the purposes of military occupation;

(ii) all democratic political parties with rights of assembly and of public discussion shall be allowed and encouraged throughout Germany;

(iii) representative and elective principles shall be introduced into regional, provincial, and state (*Land*) administration as rapidly as may be justified by the successful application of these principles in local self-government;

(iv) for the time being, no central German Government shall be established. Notwithstanding this, however, certain essential central German administrative departments, headed by State Secretaries, shall be established, particularly in the fields of finance, transport, communications, foreign trade, and industry. Such departments will act under the direction of the Control Council.

10. Subject to the necessity for maintaining military security, freedom of speech, press, and religion shall be permitted, and religious institutions shall be respected. Subject likewise to the maintenance of military security, the formation of free trade unions shall be permitted.

B. *Economic Principles*

11. In order to eliminate Germany's war potential, the production of arms, ammunition, and implements of war, as well as all types of aircraft and sea-going ships shall be prohibited and prevented. Production of metals, chemicals, machinery, and other items that are directly necessary to a war economy shall be rigidly controlled and restricted to Germany's approved postwar peacetime needs to meet the objectives stated in Paragraph 15. Productive capacity not needed for permitted production shall be removed in accordance with the reparations plan recommended by the Allied Commission on Reparations and approved by the Governments concerned or if not removed shall be destroyed.

12. At the earliest practicable date, the German economy shall be decentralized for the purpose of eliminating the present excessive concentration of economic power as exemplified in particular by cartels, syndicates, trusts and other monopolistic arrangements.

13. In organizing the German economy, primary em-

phasis shall be given to the development of agriculture and peaceful domestic industries.

14. During the period of occupation Germany shall be treated as a single economic unit. To this end common policies shall be established in regard to:

(*a*) mining and industrial production and its allocation;

(*b*) agriculture, forestry, and fishing;

(*c*) wages, prices, and rationing;

(*d*) import and export programs for Germany as a whole;

(*e*) currency and banking, central taxation and customs;

(*f*) reparation and removal of industrial war potential;

(*g*) transportation and communications.

In applying these policies account shall be taken, where appropriate, of varying local conditions.

15. Allied controls shall be imposed upon the German economy but only to the extent necessary:

(*a*) to carry out programs of industrial disarmament, demilitarization, or reparations, and of approved exports and imports.

(*b*) to assure the production and maintenance of goods and services required to meet the needs of the occupying forces and displaced persons in Germany and essential to maintain in Germany average living standards not exceeding the average of the standards of living of European countries. (European countries means all European countries excluding the United Kingdom and the U.S.S.R.)

(*c*) to ensure in the manner determined by the Control Council the equitable distribution of essential commodities between the several zones so as to produce a balanced economy throughout Germany and reduce the need for imports.

(*d*) to control German industry and all economic and financial international transactions including exports and imports, with the aim of preventing Germany from developing a war potential and of achieving the other objectives named herein.

(*e*) to control all German public or private scientific bodies, research and experimental institutions, laboratories, et cetera, connected with economic activities.

16. In the imposition and maintenance of economic controls established by the Control Council, German ad-

ministrative machinery shall be created and the German authorities shall be required to the fullest extent practicable to proclaim and assume administration of such controls. Thus it should be brought home to the German people that the responsibility for the administration of such controls and any breakdown in these controls will rest with themselves. Any German controls which may run counter to the objectives of occupation will be prohibited.

17. Measures shall be promptly taken:

(a) to effect essential repair of transport;

(b) to enlarge coal production;

(c) to maximize agricultural output; and

(d) to effect emergency repair of housing and essential utilities.

18. Appropriate steps shall be taken by the Control Council to exercise control and the power of disposition over German-owned external assets not already under control of United Nations which have taken part in the war against Germany.

19. Payment of Reparations should leave enough resources to enable the German people to subsist without external assistance. In working out the economic balance of Germany the necessary means must be provided to pay for imports approved by the Control Council in Germany. The proceeds of exports from current production and stocks shall be available in the first place for payment of such imports.

The above clause will not apply to the equipment and products referred to in paragraphs 4 (a) and 4 (b) of the Reparations Agreement.

III. REPARATIONS FROM GERMANY

1. Reparation claims of the U.S.S.R. shall be met by removals from the zone of Germany occupied by the U.S.S.R., and from appropriate German external assets.

2. The U.S.S.R. undertakes to settle the reparation claims of Poland from its own share of reparations.

3. The reparation claims of the United States, the United Kingdom and other countries entitled to reparations shall be met from the Western Zones and from appropriate German external assets.

4. In addition to the reparations to be taken by the

U.S.S.R. from its own zone of occupation, the U.S.S.R. shall receive additionally from the Western zones:

(a) 15 percent of such usable and complete industrial capital equipment, in the first place from the metallurgical, chemical and machine manufacturing industries as is unnecessary for the German peace economy and should be removed from the Western Zones of Germany, in exchange for an equivalent value of food, coal, potash, zinc, timber, clay products, petroleum products, and such other commodities as may be agreed upon.

(b) 10 percent of such industrial capital equipment as is unnecessary for the German peace economy and should be removed from the Western Zones, to be transferred to the Soviet Government on reparations account without payment or exchange of any kind in return.

Removals of equipment as provided in (a) and (b) above shall be made simultaneously.

5. The amount of the equipment to be removed from the Western Zones on account of reparations must be determined within six months from now at the latest.

6. Removals of industrial capital equipment shall begin as soon as possible and shall be completed within two years from the determination specified in paragraph 5. The delivery of products covered by 4 (a) above shall begin as soon as possible and shall be made by the U.S.S.R. in agreed installments within five years of the date hereof. The determination of the amount and character of the industrial capital equipment unnecessary for the German peace economy and therefore available for reparation shall be made by the Control Council under policies fixed by the Allied Commission on Reparations, with the participation of France, subject to the final approval of the Zone Commander from which the equipment is to be removed.

7. Prior to the fixing of the total amount of equipment subject to removal, advance deliveries shall be made in respect to such equipment as will be determined to be eligible for delivery in accordance with the procedure set forth in the last sentence of paragraph 6.

8. The Soviet Government renounces all claims in respect of reparations to shares of German enterprises which are located in the Western Zones of Germany, as well as to German foreign assets in all countries except those specified in paragraph 9 below.

9. The Governments of the U.K. and U.S.A. renounce all claims in respect of reparations to shares of German enterprises which are located in the Eastern Zone of occupation in Germany, as well as to German foreign assets in Bulgaria, Finland, Hungary, Rumania, and Eastern Austria.

10. The Soviet Government makes no claims to gold captured by the Allied troops in Germany.

IV. DISPOSAL OF THE GERMAN NAVY AND MERCHANT MARINE

A. The following principles for the distribution of the German Navy were agreed:

(1) The total strength of the German surface navy, excluding ships sunk and those taken over from Allied Nations, but including ships under construction or repair, shall be divided equally among the U.S.S.R., U.K., and U.S.A.

(2) Ships under construction or repair mean those ships whose construction or repair may be completed within three to six months according to the type of ship. Whether such ships under construction or repair shall be completed or repaired shall be determined by the technical commission appointed by the Three Powers and referred to below, subject to the principle that their completion or repair must be achieved within the time limits above provided, without any increase of skilled employment in the German shipyards and without permitting the reopening of any German shipbuilding or connected industries. Completion date means the date when a ship is able to go out on its first trip, or, under peacetime standards, would refer to the customary date of delivery by shipyard to the Government.

(3) The larger part of the German submarine fleet shall be sunk. Not more than thirty submarines shall be preserved and divided equally between the U.S.S.R., U.K., and U.S.A. for experimental and technical purposes.

(4) All stocks of armament, ammunition, and supplies of German Navy appertaining to the vessels transferred pursuant to paragraphs (1) and (3) hereof shall be handed over to the respective powers receiving such ships.

(5) The Three Governments agree to constitute a tripartite naval commission comprising two representatives

for each government, accompanied by the requisite staff, to submit agreed recommendations to the Three Governments for the allocation of specific German warships and to handle other detailed matters arising out of the agreement between the Three Governments regarding the German fleet. The Commission will hold its first meeting not later than 15th August, 1945, in Berlin, which shall be its headquarters. Each Delegation on the Commission will have the right on the basis of reciprocity to inspect German warships wherever they may be located.

(6) The Three Governments agreed that transfers, including those of ships under construction or repair, shall be completed as soon as possible, but not later than 15th February, 1946. The Commission will submit fortnightly reports, including proposals for the progressive allocation of the vessels when agreed by the Commission.

B. The following principles for the distribution of the German Merchant Marine were agreed:

(1) The German Merchant Marine, surrendered to the Three Powers and wherever located, shall be divided equally among the U.S.S.R., the U.K., and the U.S.A. The actual transfers of the ships to the respective countries shall take place as soon as practicable after the end of the war against Japan. The United Kingdom and the United States will provide out of their shares of the surrendered German merchant ships appropriate amounts for other Allied States whose merchant marines have suffered heavy losses in the common cause against Germany, except that the Soviet Union shall provide out of its share for Poland.

(2) The allocation, manning, and operation of these ships during the Japanese war period shall fall under the cognizance and authority of the Combined Shipping Adjustment Board and the United Maritime Authority.

(3) While actual transfer of the ships shall be delayed until after the end of the war with Japan, a Tripartite Shipping Commission shall inventory and value all available ships and recommend a specific distribution in accordance with paragraph (1).

(4) German inland and coastal ships determined to be necessary to the maintenance of the basic German peace economy by the Allied Control Council of Germany shall

not be included in the shipping pool thus divided among the Three Powers.

(5) The Three Governments agree to constitute a Tripartite Merchant Marine Commission comprising two representatives for each Government, accompanied by the requisite staff, to submit agreed recommendations to the Three Governments for the allocation of specific German merchant ships and to handle other detailed matters arising out of the agreement between the Three Governments regarding the German merchant ships. The Commission will hold its first meeting not later than September 1st, 1945, in Berlin, which shall be its headquarters. Each delegation on the Commission will have the right on the basis of reciprocity to inspect the German merchant ships wherever they may be located.

V. City of Koenigsberg and the Adjacent Area

The Conference examined a proposal by the Soviet Government to the effect that pending the final determination of territorial questions at the peace settlement, the section of the western frontier of the Union of Soviet Socialist Republics which is adjacent to the Baltic Sea should pass from a point on the eastern shore of the Bay of Danzig to the east, north of Braunsberg Goldap, to the meeting point of the frontiers of Lithuania, the Polish Republic, and East Prussia.

The Conference has agreed in principle to the proposal of the Soviet Government concerning the ultimate transfer to the Soviet Union of the City of Koenigsberg and the area adjacent to it as described above, subject to expert examination of the actual frontier.

The President of the United States and the British Prime Minister have declared that they will support the proposal of the Conference at the forthcoming peace settlement.

VI. War Criminals

The Three Governments have taken note of the discussions which have been proceeding in recent weeks in London between British, United States, Soviet, and French representatives with a view to reaching an agreement on the methods of trial of those major war criminals whose crimes under the Moscow Declaration of October, 1943 (*see Document No. 29*), have no particular geographical localisation. The Three Governments affirm their intention to bring these criminals to swift and sure justice. They hope that the negotiations in London will result in speedy agreement being reached for this purpose, and they regard it as a matter of great importance that the trial of these major criminals should begin at the earliest possible date. The first list of defendants will be published before 1st September.

VII. AUSTRIA

The Conference examined a proposal by the Soviet Government on the extension of the authority of the Austrian Provisional Government to all of Austria.

The Three Governments agreed that they were prepared to examine this question after the entry of the British and American forces into the city of Vienna.

It was agreed that reparations should not be exacted from Austria.

VIII. POLAND

A. *Declaration*

We have taken note with pleasure of the agreement reached among representative Poles from Poland and abroad which has made possible the formation, in accordance with the decisions reached at the Crimea Conference, of a Polish Provisional Government of National Unity recognized by the Three Powers. The establishment by the British and the United States Governments of diplomatic relations with the Polish Provisional Government of National Unity has resulted in the withdrawal of their recognition from the former Polish Government in London, which no longer exists.

The British and United States Governments have taken measures to protect the interest of the Polish Provisional Government of National Unity as the recognized government of the Polish State in the property belonging to the Polish State located in their territories and under their control, whatever the form of this property may be. They have further taken measures to prevent alienation to third parties of such property. All proper facilities will be given to the Polish Provisional Government of National Unity for the exercise of the ordinary legal remedies for the recovery of any property belonging to the Polish State which may have been wrongfully alienated.

The Three Powers are anxious to assist the Polish Provisional Government of National Unity in facilitating the return to Poland as soon as practicable of all Poles abroad who wish to go, including members of Polish Armed Forces and the Merchant Marine. They expect that those Poles who return home shall be accorded personal and property rights on the same basis as all Polish citizens.

The Three Powers note that the Polish Provisional Government of National Unity, in accordance with the decisions of the Crimea Conference, has agreed to the holding of free and unfettered elections as soon as possible on the basis of universal suffrage and secret ballot in which all democratic and anti-Nazi parties shall have the right to take part and to put forward candidates, and that the representatives of the Allied press shall enjoy full freedom to report to the world upon developments in Poland before and during the elections.

B. *Western Frontier of Poland*

In conformity with the agreement on Poland reached at the Crimea Conference the Three Heads of Government have sought the opinion of the Polish Provisional Government of National Unity in regard to the accession of territory in the north and west which Poland should receive. The President of the National Council of Poland and members of the Polish Provisional Government of National Unity have been received at the Conference and have fully presented their views. The Three Heads of Government reaffirm their opinion that the final delimitation of the western frontier of Poland should await the peace settlement.

The Three Heads of Government agree that, pending the final determination of Poland's western frontier, the former German territories east of a line running from the Baltic Sea immediately west of Swinamunde, and thence along the Oder River to the confluence of the western

Neisse River and along the western Neisse to the Czechoslovak frontier, including that portion of East Prussia not
placed under the administration of the Union of Soviet
Socialist Republics in accordance with the understanding
reached at this conference and including the area of the
former free city of Danzig, shall be under the administration of the Polish State and for such purposes should not
be considered as part of the Soviet zone of occupation in
Germany.

IX. CONCLUSION OF PEACE TREATIES AND ADMISSION TO THE UNITED NATIONS ORGANIZATION

The Three Governments consider it desirable that the
present anomalous position of Italy, Bulgaria, Finland,
Hungary, and Rumania should be terminated by the conclusion of Peace Treaties. They trust that the other interested Allied Governments will share these views.

For their part the Three Governments have included the
preparation of a Peace Treaty for Italy as the first among
the immediate important tasks to be undertaken by the
new Council of Foreign Ministers. Italy was the first of
the Axis Powers to break with Germany, to whose defeat
she has made a material contribution, and has now joined
with the Allies in the struggle against Japan. Italy has
freed herself from the Fascist regime and is making good
progress towards re-establishment of a democratic government and institutions. The conclusion of such a Peace
Treaty with a recognized and democratic Italian Government will make it possible for the Three Governments to
fulfill their desire to support an application from Italy for
membership of the United Nations.

The Three Governments have also charged the Council
of Foreign Ministers with the task of preparing Peace
Treaties for Bulgaria, Finland, Hungary, and Rumania.
The conclusion of Peace Treaties with recognized democratic governments in these States will also enable the
Three Governments to support applications from them for
membership of the United Nations. The Three Governments agree to examine each separately in the near future,
in the light of the conditions then prevailing, the establishment of diplomatic relations with Finland, Rumania, Bulgaria, and Hungary to the extent possible prior to the

conclusion of peace treaties with those countries.

The Three Governments have no doubt that in view of the changed conditions resulting from the termination of the war in Europe, representatives of the Allied press will enjoy full freedom to report to the world upon developments in Rumania, Bulgaria, Hungary, and Finland.

As regards the admission of other States into the United Nations Organization, Article 4 of the Charter of the United Nations declares that:

1. Membership in the United Nations is open to all other peace-loving States who accept the obligations contained in the present Charter and, in the judgment of the organization, are able and willing to carry out these obligations;

2. The admission of any such State to membership in the United Nations will be effected by a decision of the General Assembly upon the recommendation of the Security Council.

The Three Governments, so far as they are concerned, will support applications for membership from those States which have remained neutral during the war and which fulfill the qualifications set out above.

The Three Governments feel bound however to make it clear that they for their part would not favor any application for membership put forward by the present Spanish Government, which, having been founded with the support of the Axis Powers, does not, in view of its origins, its nature, its record, and its close association with the aggressor States possess the qualifications necessary to justify such membership.

X. TERRITORIAL TRUSTEESHIP

The Conference examined a proposal by the Soviet Government on the question of trusteeship territories as defined in the decision of the Crimea Conference and in the Charter of the United Nations Organization.

After an exchange of views on this question, it was decided that the dispositions of any former Italian colonial territories was one [sic] to be decided in connection with the preparation of a peace treaty for Italy and the question of Italian colonial territory would be considered by the September Council of Ministers of Foreign Affairs.

XI. REVISED ALLIED CONTROL COMMISSION PROCEDURE
IN RUMANIA, BULGARIA, AND HUNGARY

The Three Governments took note that the Soviet Representatives on the Allied Control Commissions in Rumania, Bulgaria, and Hungary, have communicated to their United Kingdom and United States colleagues proposals for improving the work of the Control Commissions, now that hostilities in Europe have ceased.

The Three Governments agreed that the revision of the procedures of the Allied Control Commissions in these countries would now be undertaken, taking into account the interests and responsibilities of the Three Governments, which together presented the terms of armistice to the respective countries, and accepting as a basis, in respect of all three countries, the Soviet Government's proposals for Hungary as annexed hereto. (Annex I.)

XII. ORDERLY TRANSFER OF GERMAN POPULATIONS

The Three Governments, having considered the question in all its aspects, recognize that the transfer to Germany of German populations, or elements thereof, remaining in Poland, Czechoslovakia, and Hungary, will have to be undertaken. They agree that any transfers that take place should be effected in an orderly and humane manner.

Since the influx of a large number of Germans into Germany would increase the burden already resting on the occupying authorities, they consider that the Control Council in Germany should in the first instance examine the problem, with special regard to the question of the equitable distribution of these Germans among the several zones of occupation. They are accordingly instructing their respective representatives on the Control Council to report to their Governments as soon as possible the extent to which such persons have already entered Germany from Poland, Czechoslovakia, and Hungary, and to submit an estimate of the time and rate at which further transfers could be carried out, having regard to the present situation in Germany.

The Czechoslovak Government, the Polish Provisional Government, and the Control Council in Hungary are at the same time being informed of the above and are being requested meanwhile to suspend further expulsions pending an examination by the Governments concerned of the report from their representatives on the Control Council.

XIII. Oil Equipment in Rumania

The Conference agreed to set up two bilateral commissions of experts, one to be composed of United Kingdom and Soviet Members, and one to be composed of United States and Soviet Members, to investigate the facts and examine the documents, as a basis for the settlement of questions arising from the removal of oil equipment in Rumania. It was further agreed that these experts shall begin their work within ten days, on the spot.

XIV. Iran

It was agreed that the Allied troops should be withdrawn immediately from Tehran, and that further stages of the withdrawal of troops from Iran should be considered at the meeting of the Council of Foreign Ministers to be held in London in September, 1945.

XV. The International Zone of Tangier

A proposal by the Soviet Government was examined and the following decisions were reached:

Having examined the question of the Zone of Tangier, the Three Governments have agreed that this Zone, which includes the City of Tangier and the area adjacent to it, in view of its special strategic importance, shall remain international.

The question of Tangier will be discussed in the near future at a meeting in Paris of representatives of the Governments of the Union of Soviet Socialist Republics, the United States of America, the United Kingdom and France.

XVI. The Black Sea Straits

The Three Governments recognized that the Convention concluded at Montreux[41] should be revised as failing to meet present-day conditions.

It was agreed that as the next step the matter should be the subject of direct conversations between each of the Three Governments and the Turkish Government.

[41] The Montreux Straits Convention, July 20, 1936, allowed Turkey to refortify the Straits at Constantinople.

XVII. International Inland Waterways

The Conference considered a proposal of the U. S. Delegation on this subject and agreed to refer it for consideration to the forthcoming meeting of the Council of Foreign Ministers in London.

XVIII. European Inland Transport Conference

The British and U. S. Delegations to the Conference informed the Soviet Delegation of the desire of the British and U. S. Governments to reconvene the European Inland Transport Conference and stated that they would welcome assurance that the Soviet Government would participate in the work of the reconvened conference. The Soviet Government agreed that it would participate in this conference.

XIX. Directives to Military Commanders on Allied Control Council for Germany

The Three Governments agreed that each would send a directive to its representative on the Control Council for Germany informing him of all decisions of the Conference affecting matters within the scope of his duties.

XX. Use of Allied Property for Satellite Reparations or "War Trophies"

The Proposal (Annex II) presented by the United States Delegation was accepted in principle by the Conference, but the drafting of an agreement on the matter was left to be worked out through diplomatic channels.

XXI. Military Talks

During the Conference there were meetings between the Chiefs of Staff of the Three Governments on military matters of common interest.

ANNEX I

TEXT OF A LETTER TRANSMITTED ON JULY 12 TO THE REPRESENTATIVES OF THE U. S. AND U. K. GOVERNMENTS ON THE ALLIED CONTROL COMMISSION IN HUNGARY

In view of the changed situation in connection with the

termination of the war against Germany, the Soviet Government finds it necessary to establish the following order of work for the Allied Control Commission in Hungary.

1. During the period up to the conclusion of peace with Hungary, the President (or Vice-President) of the ACC will regularly call conferences with the British and American representatives for the purpose of discussing the most important questions relating to the work of the ACC. The conferences will be called once in ten days, or more frequently in case of need.

Directives of the ACC on questions of principle will be issued to the Hungarian authorities by the President of the Allied Control Commission after agreement on these directives with the English and American representatives.

2. The British and American representatives in the ACC will take part in general conferences of heads of divisions and delegates of the ACC, convoked by the President of the ACC, which meetings will be regular in nature. The British and American representatives will also participate personally or through their representatives in appropriate instances in mixed commissions created by the President of the ACC for questions connected with the execution by the ACC of its functions.

3. Free movement by the American and British representatives in the country will be permitted provided that the ACC is previously informed of the time and route of the journeys.

4. All questions connected with permission for the entrance and exit of members of the staff of the British and American representatives in Hungary will be decided on the spot by the President of the ACC within a time limit of not more than one week.

5. The bringing in and sending out by plane of mail, cargoes, and diplomatic couriers will be carried out by the British and American representatives on the ACC under arrangements and within time limits established by the ACC, or in special cases by previous coordination with the President of the ACC.

I consider it necessary to add to the above that in all other points the existing Statutes regarding the ACC in Hungary, which was confirmed on January 20, 1945, shall remain in force in the future.

ANNEX II

USE OF ALLIED PROPERTY FOR SATELLITE REPARATIONS OR "WAR TROPHIES"

1. The burden of reparation and "war trophies" should not fall on Allied nationals.

2. *Capital Equipment.* We object to the removal of such Allied property as reparations, "war trophies," or under any other guise. Loss would accrue to Allied nationals as a result of destruction of plants and the consequent loss of markets and trading connections. Seizure of Allied property makes impossible the fulfillment by the satellite of its obligation under the armistice to restore intact the rights and interests of the Allied Nations and their Nationals.

The United States looks to the other occupying powers for the return of any equipment already removed and the cessation of removals. Where such equipment will not or cannot be returned, the U. S. will demand of the satellites adequate, effective, and prompt compensation to American nationals, and that such compensation have priority equal to that of the reparations payments.

These principles apply to all property wholly or substantially owned by Allied nationals. In the event of removals of property in which the American as well as the entire Allied interest is less than substantial, the U. S. expects adequate, effective, and prompt compensation.

3. *Current Production.* While the U. S. does not oppose reparation out of current productions of Allied investments, the satellite must provide immediate and adequate compensation to the Allied nationals including sufficient foreign exchange or products so that they can recover reasonable foreign currency expenditures and transfer a reasonable return on their investment. Such compensation must have equal priority with reparations.

We deem it essential that the satellites not conclude treaties, agreements, or arrangements which deny to Allied nationals access, on equal terms, to their trade, raw materials, and industry, and appropriately modify any existing arrangements which may have that effect.

THE FASCIST GRAND COUNCIL'S OUSTER OF MUSSOLINI, JULY 24, 1943 [42]

Following a meeting with Chancellor Adolf Hitler at which the latter refused to send heavy reinforcements to Italy in order to bolster the crumbling defenses of the Fascists, Premier Benito Mussolini called a meeting of the Fascist Grand Council, July 24, 1943. At a stormy meeting that lasted ten hours, Mussolini proposed abandoning southern Italy and continuing the war against the Allies from new headquarters in the industrial north. Instead of backing him, his erstwhile cronies, by a vote of nineteen to eight with one abstention, adopted an Order of the Day submitted by Dino Grandi and asking King Victor Emmanuel III to assume control over the kingdom. The ruler dismissed Mussolini on July 25 and appointed Marshal Pietro Badoglio as head of the government.

✓ ✓ ✓

The Grand Council,

assembled in these days of supreme trial, turns its thought first of all to the heroic fighters of every branch of the forces, who side by side with the proud people of Sicily, among whom the single-minded faith of the Italian people shines most brightly, are renewing the noble traditions of arduous courage and the indomitable spirit of sacrifice of our glorious armed forces; proclaims it to be the sacred duty of all Italians to defend at all costs the unity, independence, and liberty of the country, the fruits of the sacri-

---

[42] D. Alfieri, *Due dittatori di fronte* (Rizzoli, Milan, 1946), p. 331, as translated in Royal Institute of Foreign Affairs, *Documents on International Affairs 1939-1946*, II, *Hitler's Europe*, ed. by Margaret Carlyle (Oxford University Press, London, 1954), p. 118. Reprinted by permission.

fices and efforts of four generations from the Risorgimento
till today, and the life and future of the Italian people;
affirms the need for the moral and physical union of all
Italians at this serious moment which is decisive for the
destiny of the nation;

declares that to achieve this unity it is necessary to restore
immediately all functions belonging to the state, ascribing
to the Crown, the Grand Council, the Government, Parliament, and the Corporations the tasks and responsibilities
laid down for them by our state and constitutional laws;
invites the Head of the Government to pray His Majesty
the King, to whom the faithful and trusting heart of the
whole Nation turns, that for the honour and safety of the
country he now assume effective command of the armed
forces on land, on sea, and in the air, in accordance with
Article 5 of the Statute of the Kingdom, and therewith the
supreme initiative of decision which our institutions attribute to him, and which have always been throughout
our national history the glorious appendage of our august
dynasty of the House of Savoy.

— 35 —

THE ITALIAN ARMISTICE, SEPTEMBER 3, 1943 [43]

*When Marshal Pietro Badoglio became Head of the
Italian Government on July 25, 1943, he continued the war
against the Allies, in part because the Germans were in
occupation of so much of Italy. But the stepped-up
Allied air attacks and the outbreak of peace riots in several cities, soon led Badoglio, in secret, to request an*

[43] United States, Department of State, *Bulletin* (Government
Printing Office, Washington, 1945), XIII, 748.

armistice. His agents met representatives of General Dwight D. Eisenhower in Lisbon, Portugal, and on September 3, 1943, Italy surrendered unconditionally. The news was made public on September 8, and on October 13, 1943, Italy declared war on Nazi Germany. The "Short Armistice" of September 3 was modified by a lengthy and detailed protocol signed November 9, 1943.

✦   ✦   ✦

The following conditions of an Armistice are presented by General Dwight D. Eisenhower, Commander-in-Chief of the Allied Forces, acting by authority of the Governments of the United States and Great Britain and in the interest of the United Nations, and are accepted by

Marshal Pietro Badoglio

Head of the Italian Government.

1. Immediate cessation of all hostile activity by the Italian armed forces.

2. Italy will use its best endeavors to deny, to the Germans, facilities that might be used against the United Nations.

3. All prisoners or internees of the United Nations to be immediately turned over to the Allied Commander-in-Chief, and none of these may now or at any time be evacuated to Germany.

4. Immediate transfer of the Italian Fleet and Italian aircraft to such points as may be designated by the Allied Commander-in-Chief, with details of disarmament to be prescribed by him.

5. Italian merchant shipping may be requisitioned by the Allied Commander-in-Chief to meet the needs of his military-naval program.

6. Immediate surrender of Corsica and of all Italian territory, both islands and mainland, to the Allies, for such use as operational bases and other purposes as the Allies may see fit.

7. Immediate guarantee of the free use by the Allies of all airfields and naval ports in Italian territory, regardless of the rate of evacuation of the Italian territory by the German forces. These ports and fields to be protected by Italian armed forces until this function is taken over by the Allies.

8. Immediate withdrawal to Italy of Italian armed

forces from all participation in the current war from whatever areas in which they may now be engaged.

9. Guarantee by the Italian Government that if necessary it will employ all its available armed forces to insure prompt and exact compliance with all the provisions of this armistice.

10. The Commander-in-Chief of the Allied Forces reserves to himself the right to take any measure which in his opinion may be necessary for the protection of the interests of the Allied Forces for the prosecution of the war, and the Italian Government binds itself to take such administrative or other action as the Commander-in-Chief may require, and in particular the Commander-in-Chief will establish Allied Military Government over such parts of Italian territory as he may deem necessary in the military interests of the Allied Nations.

11. The Commander-in-Chief of the Allied Forces will have a full right to impose measures of disarmament, demobilization, and demilitarization.

12. Other conditions of a political, economic, and financial nature with which Italy will be bound to comply will be transmitted at later date.

The conditions of the present Armistice will not be made public without prior approval of the Allied Commander-in-Chief. The English will be considered the official text.

MARCHAL PIETRO BADOGLIO
*Head of the Italian
Government*

DWIGHT D. EISENHOWER
*General, U. S. Army
Commander-in-Chief
Allied Forces*

by:
GIUSEPPE CASTELLANO
*Brigadier General,
attached to the Italian
High Command*

by:
WALTER B. SMITH
*Major General,
U. S. Army
Chief of Staff*

THE PRIVATE AND POLITICAL TESTAMENTS OF HITLER, APRIL 29, 1945 [44]

With Berlin under Russian siege, Chancellor Adolf Hitler on April 29, 1945, married his companion Eva Braun and wrote two wills. On the next day he shot himself, his wife swallowed poison, and both bodies were buried in the Chancellery garden. The wills apparently were reproduced in several copies and one set was sent by Hitler's secretary, Martin Bormann, to Grand Admiral Karl Doenitz, designated in the testament as "President of the Reich."

✓   ✓   ✓

My Private Will and Testament

As I did not consider that I could take responsibility, during the years of struggle, of contracting a marriage, I have now decided, before the closing of my earthly career, to take as my wife that girl who, after many years of faithful friendship, entered, of her own free will, the practically besieged town in order to share her destiny with me. At her own desire she goes as my wife with me into death. It will compensate us for what we both lost through my work in the service of my people.

What I possess belongs—insofar as it has any value— to the Party. Should this no longer exist, to the State; should the State also be destroyed, no further decision of mine is necessary.

[44] United States, Office of United States Chief of Counsel for Prosecution of Axis Criminality, *Nazi Conspiracy and Aggression,* 8 vols. and 2 suppl. vols. (Government Printing Office, Washington, 1946-1948), VI, 259-263, Doc. No. 3569-PS.

My pictures, in the collections which I have bought in the course of years, have never been collected for private purposes, but only for the extension of a gallery in my home town of Linz a.d. Donau.

It is my most sincere wish that this bequest may be duly executed.

I nominate as my Executor my most faithful Party comrade,

Martin Bormann

He is given full legal authority to make all decisions. He is permitted to take out everything that has a sentimental value or is necessary for the maintenance of a modest simple life, for my brothers and sisters, also above all for the mother of my wife and my faithful co-workers who are well known to him, principally my old Secretaries Frau Winter, etc. who have for many years aided me by their work.

I myself and my wife—in order to escape the disgrace of deposition or capitulation—choose death. It is our wish to be burnt immediately on the spot where I have carried out the greatest part of my daily work in the course of a twelve years' service to my people.

Given in Berlin, 29th April 1945, 4:00 o'clock

(*Signed*) A. HITLER

My Political Testament

More than thirty years have now passed since I in 1914 made my modest contribution as a volunteer in the first world war that was forced upon the Reich.

In these three decades I have been actuated solely by love and loyalty to my people in all my thoughts, acts, and life. They gave me the strength to make the most difficult decisions which have ever confronted mortal man. I have spent my time, my working strength, and my health in these three decades.

It is untrue that I or anyone else in Germany wanted the war in 1939. It was desired and instigated exclusively by those international statesmen who were either of Jewish descent or worked for Jewish interests. I have made too many offers for the control and limitation of armaments, which posterity will not for all time be able to disregard for the responsibility for the outbreak of this war to be laid on me. I have further never wished that after the first fatal world war a second against England, or even against America, should break out. Centuries will pass away, but out of the ruins of our towns and monuments the hatred against those finally responsible whom we have to thank for everything, international Jewry and its helpers, will grow.

Three days before the outbreak of the German-Polish war I again proposed to the British ambassador in Berlin a solution to the German-Polish problem—similar to that in the case of the Saar district, under international control. This offer also cannot be denied. It was only rejected because the leading circles in English politics wanted the war, partly on account of the business hoped for and partly under influence of propaganda organized by international Jewry.

I have also made it quite plain that, if the nations of Europe are again to be regarded as mere shares to be bought and sold by these international conspirators in money and finance, then that race, Jewry, which is the real criminal of this murderous struggle, will be saddled with the responsibility. I further left no one in doubt that this time not only would millions of children of Europe's Aryan peoples die of hunger, not only would millions of grown men suffer death, and not only hundreds of thousands of women and children be burnt and bombed to death in the towns, without the real criminal having to atone for this guilt, even if by more humane means.

After six years of war, which in spite of all setbacks, will go down one day in history as the most glorious and valiant demonstration of a nation's life purpose, I cannot forsake the city which is the capital of this Reich. As the forces are too small to make any further stand against the enemy attack at this place, and our resistance is gradually being weakened by men who are as deluded as they are lacking in initiative, I should like, by remaining in this town, to share my fate with those, the millions of others, who have also taken upon themselves to do so. Moreover I do not wish to fall into the hands of an enemy who requires a new spectacle organized by the Jews for the amusement of their hysterical masses.

I have decided therefore to remain in Berlin and there

of my own free will to choose death at the moment when I believe the position of the Fuehrer and Chancellor itself can no longer be held.

I die with a happy heart, aware of the immeasurable deeds and achievements of our soldiers at the front, our women at home, the achievements of our farmers and workers and the work, unique in history, of our youth who bear my name.

That from the bottom of my heart I express my thanks to you all, is just as self-evident as my wish that you should, because of that, on no account give up the struggle, but rather continue it against the enemies of the Fatherland, no matter where, true to the creed of a great Clausewitz. From the sacrifice of our soldiers and from my own unity with them unto death, will in any case spring up in the history of Germany, the seed of a radiant renaissance of the National-Socialist movement and thus of the realization of a true community of nations.

Many of the most courageous men and women have decided to unite their lives with mine until the very last. I have begged and finally ordered them not to do this, but to take part in the further battle of the Nation. I beg the heads of the Armies, the Navy, and the Air Force to strengthen by all possible means the spirit of resistance of our soldiers in the National-Socialist sense, with special reference to the fact that also I myself, as founder and creator of this movement, have preferred death to cowardly abdication or even capitulation.

May it, at some future time, become part of the code of honour of the German officer—as is already the case in our Navy—that the surrender of a district or of a town is impossible, and that above all the leaders here must march ahead as shining examples, faithfully fulfilling their duty unto death.

Second Part of the Political Testament

Before my death I expel the former Reichsmarschall Hermann Goering from the party and deprive him of all rights which he may enjoy by virtue of the decree of June 29th, 1941; and also by virtue of my statement in the Reichstag on September 1st, 1939, I appoint in his place Grossadmiral Doenitz, President of the Reich and Supreme Commander of the Armed Forces.

Before my death I expel the former Reichsfuehrer-SS and Minister of the Interior, Heinrich Himmler, from the party and from all offices of State. In his stead I appoint Gauleiter Karl Hanke as Reichsfuehrer-SS and Chief of the German Police, and Gauleiter Paul Giesler as Reich Minister of the Interior.

Goering and Himmler, quite apart from their disloyalty to my person, have done immeasurable harm to the country and the whole nation by secret negotiations with the enemy, which they conducted without my knowledge and against my wishes, and by illegally attempting to seize power in the State for themselves.

In order to give the German people a government composed of honourable men,—a government which will fulfill its pledge to continue the war by every means—I appoint the following members of the new Cabinet as leaders of the nation:

President of the Reich:	DOENITZ
Chancellor of the Reich:	DR. GOEBBELS
Party Minister:	BORMANN
Foreign Minister:	SEYSS-INQUART

[*Here follow fifteen others.*]

Although a number of these men, such as Martin Bormann, Dr. Goebbels, etc., together with their wives, have joined me of their own free will and did not wish to leave the capital of the Reich under any circumstances, but were willing to perish with me here, I must nevertheless ask them to obey my request, and in this case set the interests of the nation above their own feelings. By their work and loyalty as comrades they will be just as close to me after death, as I hope that my spirit will linger among them and always go with them. Let them be hard, but never unjust, above all let them never allow fear to influence their actions, and set the honour of the nation above everything in the world. Finally, let them be conscious of the fact that our task, that of continuing the building of a National Socialist State, represents the work of the coming centuries, which places every single person under an obligation always to serve the common interest and to subordinate his own advantage to this end. I demand of all Germans, all National Socialists, men, women, and all the men of the Armed Forces, that they be faithful and obedient unto death to the new government and its President.

Above all I charge the leaders of the nation and those under them to scrupulous observance of the laws of race and to merciless opposition to the universal poisoner of all peoples, international Jewry.

Given in Berlin, this 29th day of April 1945. 4:00 A.M.

ADOLF HITLER

— 37 —

ASSUMPTION OF POWER BY DOENITZ, MAY 1, 1945 [45]

On May 1, 1945, Grand Admiral Karl Doenitz informed the world by radio that he had assumed the late Fuehrer's mantle as head of the German nation and Commander-in-Chief of its armed forces.

1   1   1

German men and women, soldiers of the German armed forces. Our Fuehrer Adolf Hitler is dead. The German people bow in deepest sorrow and respect. Early he had recognized the terrible danger of Bolshevism and had dedicated his life to the fight against it. His fight having ended, he died a hero's death in the capital of the German Reich, after having led a straight and steady life.

His life was dedicated to the service of Germany. His devotion in the fight against the Bolshevist flood was in

[45] United States, Office of United States Chief of Counsel for Prosecution of Axis Criminality, *Nazi Conspiracy and Aggression,* 8 vols. and 2 suppl. vols. (Government Printing Office, Washington, 1946-1948), VII, 56, Doc. No. D-444.

the interest not only of Europe but of the entire civilized world. The Fuehrer has nominated me as his successor. Fully conscious of the responsibility, I am taking over the leadership of the German nation in this fateful hour; my first task is to save German men from being destroyed by the advancing Bolshevist enemy. For this reason only do the Armies continue fighting. As far and as long as the achievement of this task is being prevented by the British and Americans, we have to defend ourselves against them too and must go on fighting. Thus the Anglo-Americans are no longer carrying on the fight for their own peoples but only for the spreading of Bolshevism in Europe. What the German people have achieved in this war through fighting and [the] sufferings they have undergone at home are unique in history. In the coming emergency arising for our people I shall to the best of my ability make it my business to secure for our brave women, men, and children the most tolerable conditions essential to life.

In order to do this, I need your help. Give me your confidence, as your road is also my road. Uphold order and discipline in towns and country. Let everybody remain at his post doing his duty. Only thus will we be able to mitigate the suffering, which the future will bring for every one of us, and prevent the collapse. If we do all that is in our power, God will not forsake us after so much suffering and sacrifice.

— 38 —

THE GERMAN SURRENDER, MAY 7-8/9, 1945 [46]

[46] *A* and *B* are from United States, Department of State, Publication No. 2423, *The Axis in Defeat. A Collection of Documents on American Policy toward Germany and Japan* (Government Printing Office, Washington, n.d. [1945]), pp. 23-25.

Six days after he succeeded the Fuehrer, Grand Admiral Karl Doenitz agreed to Germany's unconditional surrender. His emissary, Colonel General Alfred Jodl, signed the act of surrender in a Reims schoolhouse on May 7, 1945 (V-E or Victory-in-Europe Day). The U.S.S.R. insisted on a second surrender ceremony in Berlin on May 8 (May 9, Russian time). A Soviet film of this second surrender contained no reference to the earlier capitulation at Reims.

↗   ↗   ↗

A

Only this text in English is authoritative.

ACT OF MILITARY SURRENDER

1. We the undersigned, acting by authority of the German High Command, hereby surrender unconditionally to the Supreme Commander, Allied Expeditionary Force and simultaneously to the Soviet High Command all forces on land, sea, and in the air who are at this date under German control.

2. The German High Command will at once issue orders to all German military, naval, and air authorities and to all forces under German control to cease active operations at 2301 hours Central European time on 8 May and to remain in the positions occupied at that time. No ship, vessel, or aircraft is to be scuttled, or any damage done to their hull, machinery, or equipment.

3. The German High Command will at once issue to the appropriate commanders, and ensure the carrying out of any further orders issued by the Supreme Commander, Allied Expeditionary Force and by the Soviet High Command.

4. This act of military surrender is without prejudice to, and will be superseded by, any general instrument of surrender imposed by, or on behalf of, the United Nations and applicable to GERMANY and the German armed forces as a whole.

5. In the event of the German High Command or any of the forces under their control failing to act in accordance with this Act of Surrender, the Supreme Commander, Allied Expeditionary Force and the Soviet High

Command will take such punitive or other action as they deem appropriate.

Signed at Rheims at 0241 on the 7th day of May, 1945
On behalf of the German High Command.

JODL

IN THE PRESENCE OF:

On behalf of the
Supreme Commander,
Allied Expeditionary Force
   W. B. SMITH
	On behalf of the
	Soviet High Command
	   SOUSLOPAROV

F. SEVEZ
Major General, French Army (Witness)

B

ACT OF MILITARY SURRENDER

1. We the undersigned, acting by authority of the German High Command, hereby surrender unconditionally to the Supreme Commander, Allied Expeditionary Force and simultaneously to the Supreme High Command of the Red Army all forces on land, at sea, and in the air who are at this date under German control.

2. The German High Command will at once issue orders to all German military, naval, and air authorities and to all forces under German control to cease active operations at 2301 hours Central European time on 8th May, 1945, to remain in the positions occupied at that time and to disarm completely, handing over their weapons and equipment to the local allied commanders or officers designated by Representatives of the Allied Supreme Commands. No ship, vessel, or aircraft is to be scuttled, or any damage done to their hull, machinery, or equipment, and also to machines of all kinds, armament, apparatus, and all the technical means of prosecution of war in general.

3. The German High Command will at once issue to the appropriate commanders, and ensure the carrying out of, any further orders issued by the Supreme Commander, Allied Expeditionary Force and by the Supreme High Command of the Red Army.

4. This act of military surrender is without prejudice to, and will be superseded by, any general instrument of surrender imposed by, or on behalf of, the United Nations and applicable to GERMANY and the German armed forces as a whole.

5. In the event of the German High Command or any of the forces under their control failing to act in accordance with this Act of Surrender, the Supreme Commander, Allied Expeditionary Force and the Supreme High Command of the Red Army will take such punitive or other action as they deem appropriate.

6. This Act is drawn up in the English, Russian, and German languages. The English and Russian are the only authentic texts.

Signed at Berlin on the 8th day of May, 1945

FRIEDEBURG; KEITEL; STUMPFF
On behalf of the German High Command

IN THE PRESENCE OF:

On behalf of the
Supreme Commander
Allied Expeditionary Force
  A. W. TEDDER

On behalf of
Supreme High Command
of the Red Army
  G. ZHUKOV

At the signing also were present as witnesses:

F. DE LATTRE-TASSIGNY
General,
Commander-in-Chief
First French Army

CARL SPAATZ
General, Commanding
United States Strategic
Air Forces

— 39 —

THE ATOMIC BOMBING OF
HIROSHIMA, AUGUST 6, 1945 [47]

*One of the decisions reached at the Potsdam Confer-
ence (see Document No. 33) was to try to shorten the
war by dropping an atomic bomb on a Japanese target.
On August 6, 1945, a United States bomber destroyed
more than half of the militarily important city of Hiroshima by means of a small bomb operating through atomic
fission.*

↗   ↗   ↗

STATEMENT BY THE PRESIDENT
OF THE UNITED STATES

August 6, 1945
The White House
Washington, D.C.

Sixteen hours ago an American airplane dropped one
bomb on Hiroshima, an important Japanese Army base.
That bomb had more power than 20,000 tons of T.N.T.
It had more than two thousand times the blast power of
the British "Grand Slam," which is the largest bomb ever
yet used in the history of warfare.

The Japanese began the war from the air at Pearl Harbor. They have been repaid many fold. And the end is not
yet. With this bomb we have now added a new and revo-
lutionary increase in destruction to supplement the growing power of our armed forces. In their present forms
these bombs are now in production and even more powerful forms are in development.

[47] United States, Department of State, Publication No. 2702,
*The International Control of Atomic Energy. Growth of a
Policy* (Government Printing Office, Washington, n.d.
[1947]), pp. 95-97.

It is an atomic bomb. It is a harnessing of the basic power of the universe. The force from which the sun draws its power has been loosed against those who brought war to the Far East.

Before 1939, it was the accepted belief of scientists that it was theoretically possible to release atomic energy. But no one knew any practical method of doing it. By 1942, however, we knew that the Germans were working feverishly to find a way to add atomic energy to the other engines of war with which they hoped to enslave the world. But they failed. We may be grateful to Providence that the Germans got the V-1's and the V-2's late and in limited quantities and even more grateful that they did not get the atomic bomb at all.

The battle of the laboratories held fateful risks for us as well as the battles of the air, land, and sea, and we have now won the battle of the laboratories as we have won the other battles.

Beginning in 1940, before Pearl Harbor, scientific knowledge useful in war was pooled between the United States and Great Britain, and many priceless helps to our victories have come from that arrangement. Under that general policy the research on the atomic bomb was begun. With American and British scientists working together we entered the race of discovery against the Germans.

The United States had available the large number of scientists of distinction in the many needed areas of knowledge. It had the tremendous industrial and financial resources necessary for the project and they could be devoted to it without undue impairment of other vital war work. In the United States the laboratory work and the production plants, on which a substantial start had already been made, would be out of reach of enemy bombing, while at that time Britain was exposed to constant air attack and was still threatened with the possibility of invasion. For these reasons Prime Minister Churchill and President Roosevelt agreed that it was wise to carry on the project here. We now have two great plants and many lesser works devoted to the production of atomic power. Employment during peak construction numbered 125,000 and over 65,000 individuals are even now engaged in operating the plants. Many have worked there for two and a half years. Few know what they have been producing.

They see great quantities of material going in and they see nothing coming out of these plants, for the physical size of the explosive charge is exceedingly small. We have spent two billion dollars on the greatest scientific gamble in history—and won.

But the greatest marvel is not the size of the enterprise, its secrecy, nor its cost, but the achievement of scientific brains in putting together infinitely complex pieces of knowledge held by many men in different fields of science into a workable plan. And hardly less marvelous has been the capacity of industry to design, and of labor to operate, the machines and methods to do things never done before so that the brain child of many minds came forth in physical shape and performed as it was supposed to do. Both science and industry worked under the direction of the United States Army, which achieved a unique success in managing so diverse a problem in the advancement of knowledge in an amazingly short time. It is doubtful if such another combination could be got together in the world. What has been done is the greatest achievement of organized science in history. It was done under high pressure and without failure.

We are now prepared to obliterate more rapidly and completely every productive enterprise the Japanese have above ground in any city. We shall destroy their docks, their factories, and their communications. Let there be no mistakes; we shall completely destroy Japan's power to make war.

It was to spare the Japanese people from utter destruction that the ultimatum of July 26 was issued at Potsdam. Their leaders promptly rejected that ultimatum. If they do not now accept our terms, they may expect a rain of ruin from the air, the like of which has never been seen on this earth. Behind this air attack will follow sea and land forces in such numbers and power as they have not yet seen and with the fighting skill of which they are already well aware.

The Secretary of War, who has kept in personal touch with all phases of the project, will immediately make public a statement giving further details.

His statement will give facts concerning the sites at Oak Ridge near Knoxville, Tennessee, and at Richland near Pasco, Washington, and an installation near Santa

Fe, New Mexico. Although the workers at the sites have been making materials to be used in producing the greatest destructive force in history, they have not themselves been in danger beyond that of many other occupations, for the utmost care has been taken for their safety.

The fact that we can release atomic energy ushers in a new era in man's understanding of nature's forces. Atomic energy may in the future supplement the power that now comes from coal, oil, and falling water, but at present it cannot be produced on a basis to compete with them commercially. Before that comes, there must be a long period of intensive research.

It has never been the habit of the scientists of this country or the policy of this Government to withhold from the world scientific knowledge. Normally, therefore, everything about the work with atomic energy would be made public.

But under present circumstances it is not intended to divulge the technical processes of production or all the military applications, pending further examination of possible methods of protecting us and the rest of the world from the danger of sudden destruction.

I shall recommend that the Congress of the United States consider promptly the establishment of an appropriate commission to control the production and use of atomic power within the United States. I shall give further consideration and make further recommendations to the Congress as to how atomic power can become a powerful and forceful influence towards the maintenance of world peace.

— 40 —

THE SURRENDER OF JAPAN, SEPTEMBER 2, 1945 [48]

Moscow declared war on Tokyo two days after the atomic bombing of Hiroshima. (See Document No. 39.) Nagasaki was similarly bombed on August 9. One day later—after the Soviet Union had been Japan's enemy only four days and had done almost no fighting—the Japanese sued for peace. A document of unconditional surrender was signed aboard the U.S.S. Missouri *in Tokyo Bay on September 2, 1945 (V-J or Victory-over-Japan Day).*

✓   ✓   ✓

INSTRUMENT OF SURRENDER

We, acting by command of and in behalf of the Emperor of Japan, the Japanese Government and the Japanese Imperial General Headquarters, hereby accept the provisions set forth in the declaration issued by the heads of the Governments of the United States, China, and Great Britain on 26 July, 1945 at Potsdam, and subsequently adhered to by the Union of Soviet Socialist Republics, which four powers are hereafter referred to as the Allied Powers.

We hereby proclaim the unconditional surrender to the Allied Powers of the Japanese Imperial General Headquarters and of all Japanese armed forces and all armed forces under Japanese control wherever situated.

We hereby command all Japanese forces wherever situated and the Japanese people to cease hostilities forth-

[48] *Report of Government Section [of General Headquarters] Supreme Commander for the Allied Powers, Political Reorientation of Japan September 1945 to September 1948,* 2 vols. (Government Printing Office, Washington, n.d. [1950]), II, 419.

with, to preserve and save from damage all ships, aircraft, and military and civil property and to comply with all requirements which may be imposed by the Supreme Commander for the Allied Powers or by agencies of the Japanese Government at his direction.

We hereby command the Japanese Imperial General Headquarters to issue at once orders to the Commanders of all Japanese forces and all forces under Japanese control wherever situated to surrender unconditionally themselves and all forces under their control.

We hereby command all civil, military, and naval officials to obey and enforce all proclamations, orders, and directives deemed by the Supreme Commander for the Allied Powers to be proper to effectuate this surrender and issued by him or under his authority, and we direct all such officials to remain at their posts and to continue to perform their noncombatant duties unless specifically relieved by him or under his authority.

We hereby undertake for the Emperor, the Japanese Government, and their successors to carry out the provisions of the Potsdam Declaration in good faith, and to issue whatever orders and take whatever action may be required by the Supreme Commander for the Allied Powers or by any other designated representatives of the Allied Powers for the purpose of giving effect to that Declaration.

We hereby command the Japanese Imperial Government and the Japanese Imperial General Headquarters at once to liberate all allied prisoners of war and civilian internees now under Japanese control and to provide for their protection, care, maintenance, and immediate transportation to places as directed.

The authority of the Emperor and the Japanese Government to rule the state shall be subject to the Supreme Commander for the Allied Powers, who will take such steps as he deems proper to effectuate these terms of surrender.

Signed at Tokyo Bay, Japan at 0904 on the Second day of September, 1945.

(*Signed*) MAMORU SHIGEMITSU
          By command and in behalf of the Emperor of Japan and the Japanese Government

(*Signed*) YOSHIJIRO UMEZU
> *By Command and in behalf of the Japanese
> Imperial General Headquarters*

Accepted at Tokyo Bay, Japan at 0908 on the Second day of September, 1945, for the United States, Republic of China, United Kingdom, and the Union of Soviet Socialist Republics, and in the interests of the other United Nations at war with Japan.

(*Signed*) DOUGLAS MACARTHUR,
> *Supreme Commander for the Allied Powers*

(*Signed*) C. W. NIMITZ
> *United States Representative*

(*Signed*) HSU YUNG-CHANG
> *Republic of China Representative*

(*Signed*) BRUCE FRASER
> *United Kingdom Representative*

(*Signed*) LIEUT. GEN. K. DEREVYANKO
> *Union of Soviet Socialist Republics
> Representative*

— 41 —

SERVICEMEN'S READJUSTMENT ACT OF 1944, JUNE 22, 1944 [49]

On June 22, 1944, Congress passed "An Act to provide Federal Government aid for the readjustment in civilian life of returning World War II veterans." This "G.I. Bill of Rights" extended federal financial aid to veterans who wished to continue their education or who wanted to purchase houses or set up small businesses, provided free medical services to veterans and their families, and

[49] *United States Statutes at Large* (Government Printing Office, Washington, 1944), LVII, 284 ff.

granted unemployment benefits to ex-servicemen out of work. Known also as Public Law 346, the act made the transition from war to peace easier for millions, encouraged many who otherwise would not have done so to continue their education, and prevented a dangerously rapid swelling of the postwar labor market. The "Education of Veterans" was covered by Chapter IV of the law.

✓   ✓   ✓

Part VIII

1. Any person who served in the active military or naval service on or after September 16, 1940, and prior to the termination of the present war, and who shall have been discharged or released therefrom under conditions other than dishonorable, and whose education or training was impeded, delayed, interrupted, or interfered with by reason of his entrance into the service, or who desires a refresher or retraining course, and who either shall have served ninety days or more, exclusive of any period he was assigned for a course of education or training under the Army specialized training program or the Navy college training program, which course was a continuation of his civilian course and was pursued to completion, or as a cadet or midshipman at one of the service academies, or shall have been discharged or released from active service by reason of an actual service-incurred injury or disability, shall be eligible for, and entitled to receive, education or training under this part: *Provided,* That such course shall be initiated not later than two years after either the date of his discharge or the termination of the present war, whichever is the later: *Provided further,* That no such education or training shall be afforded beyond seven years after the termination of the present war: *And provided further,* That any such person who was not over 25 years of age at the time he entered the service shall be deemed to have had his education or training impeded, delayed, interrupted, or interfered with.

2. Any such eligible person shall be entitled to education or training, or a refresher or retraining course, at an approved educational or training institution, for a period of one year (or the equivalent thereof in continuous part-time study), or for such lesser time as may be required

for the course of instruction chosen by him. Upon satisfactory completion of such course of education or training, according to the regularly prescribed standards and practices of the institutions, except a refresher or retraining course, such person shall be entitled to an additional period or periods of education or training, not to exceed the time such person was in the active service on or after September 16, 1940, and before the termination of the war, exclusive of any period he was assigned for a course of education or training under the Army specialized training program or the Navy college training program, which course was a continuation of his civilian course and was pursued to completion, or as a cadet or midshipman at one of the service academies, but in no event shall the total period of education or training exceed four years: *Provided,* That his work continues to be satisfactory throughout the period, according to the regularly prescribed standards and practices of the institution: *Provided, however,* That wherever the additional period of instruction ends during a quarter or semester and after a major part of such quarter or semester has expired, such period of instruction shall be extended to the termination of such unexpired quarter or semester.

3. Such person shall be eligible for, and entitled to, such course of education or training as he may elect, and at any approved educational or training institution at which he chooses to enroll, whether or not located in the State in which he resides, which will accept or retain him as a student or trainee in any field or branch of knowledge which such institution finds him qualified to undertake or pursue: *Provided,* That, for reasons satisfactory to the Administrator, he may change a course of instruction: *And provided further,* That any such course of education or training may be discontinued at any time, if it is found by the Administrator that, according to the regularly prescribed standards and practices of the institution, the conduct or progress of such person is unsatisfactory. . . .

6. While enrolled in and pursuing a course under this part, such person, upon application to the Administrator, shall be paid a subsistence allowance of $50 per month, if without a dependent or dependents, or $75 per month, if he has a dependent or dependents, including regular holi-

days and leave not exceeding thirty days in a calendar year. Such person attending a course on a part-time basis, and such person receiving compensation for productive labor performed as part of their apprentice or other training on the job at institutions, business or other establishments, shall be entitled to receive such lesser sums, if any, as subsistence or dependency allowances, as may be determined by the Administrator: *Provided,* That any such person eligible under this part, and within the limitations thereof, may pursue such full time or part-time course or courses as he may elect, without subsistence allowance. . . .

8. No department, agency, or officer of the United States, in carrying out the provisions of this part, shall exercise any supervision or control, whatsoever, over any State educational agency, or State apprenticeship agency, or any educational or training institution: *Provided,* That nothing in this section shall be deemed to prevent any department, agency, or officer of the United States from exercising any supervision or control which such department, agency, or officer is authorized, by existing provisions of law, to exercise over any Federal educational or training institution, or to prevent the furnishing of education or training under this part in any institution over which supervision or control is exercised by such other department, agency, or officer under authority of existing provisions of law. . . .

11. As used in this part, the term "educational or training institutions" shall include all public or private elementary, secondary, and other schools furnishing education for adults, business schools and colleges, scientific and technical institutions, colleges, vocational schools, junior colleges, teachers colleges, normal schools, professional schools, universities, and other educational institutions, and shall also include business or other establishments providing apprentice or other training on the job. . . .

42

DIRECTIVE TO EISENHOWER ON GERMAN MILITARY GOVERNMENT, APRIL, 1945 AND OCTOBER 17, 1945 [50]

The United States Joint Chiefs of Staff in April, 1945 sent General Dwight D. Eisenhower a basic directive (JCS/1067) on the military occupation of Germany. Its provisions had some influence on the decisions reached at the Potsdam Conference (see Document No. 33) ; *the latter, in turn, modified some of the Directive's original clauses. The Directive, as made public on October 17, 1945, contained these revisions.*

✓   ✓   ✓

DIRECTIVE TO COMMANDER-IN-CHIEF OF UNITED STATES FORCES OF OCCUPATION REGARDING THE MILITARY GOVERNMENT OF GERMANY

1. *The Purpose and Scope of this Directive:*

This directive is issued to you as Commanding General of the United States forces of occupation in Germany. As such you will serve as United States member of the Control Council and will also be responsible for the administration of military government in the zone or zones assigned to the United States for purposes of occupation and administration. It outlines the basic policies which will guide you in those two capacities after the ter-

[50] United States, Department of State, Publication No. 2423, *The Axis in Defeat. A Collection of Documents on American Policy toward Germany and Japan* (Government Printing Office, Washington, n.d. [1945]), pp. 40-59.

mination of the combined command of the Supreme Commander, Allied Expeditionary Force.

This directive sets forth policies relating to Germany in the initial post-defeat period. As such it is not intended to be an ultimate statement of policies of this Government concerning the treatment of Germany in the postwar world. It is therefore essential that, during the period covered by this directive, you assure that surveys are constantly maintained of economic, industrial, financial, social, and political conditions within your zone and that the results of such surveys and such other surveys as may be made in other zones are made available to your Government, through the Joint Chiefs of Staff. These surveys should be developed in such manner as to serve as a basis for determining changes in the measures of control set forth herein, as well as for the progressive formulation and development of policies to promote the basic objectives of the United States. Supplemental directives will be issued to you by the Joint Chiefs of Staff as may be required.

As a member of the Control Council, you will urge the adoption by the other occupying powers of the principles and policies set forth in this directive and, pending Control Council agreement, you will follow them in your zone. It is anticipated that substantially similar directives will be issued to the Commanders-in-Chief of the U.K., U.S.S.R., and French forces of occupation.

PART I

GENERAL AND POLITICAL

2. *The Basis of Military Government:*

a. The rights, power, and status of the military government in Germany are based upon the unconditional surrender or total defeat of Germany.

b. Subject to the provisions of paragraph 3 below, you are, by virtue of your position, clothed with supreme legislative, executive, and judicial authority in the areas occupied by forces under your command. This authority will be broadly construed and includes authority to take all measures deemed by you necessary, appropriate, or desirable in relation to military exigencies and the objectives of a firm military government.

c. You will issue a proclamation continuing in force such proclamations, orders, and instructions as may have heretofore been issued by Allied Commanders in your zone, subject to such changes as you may determine. Authorizations of action by the Supreme Commander, Allied Expeditionary Force, may be considered as applicable to you unless inconsistent with this or later directives.

3. *The Control Council and Zones of Occupation:*

a. The four Commanders-in-Chief, acting jointly, will constitute the Control Council in Germany which will be the supreme organ of control over Germany in accordance with the agreement on Control Machinery in Germany. For purposes of administration of military government, Germany has been divided into four zones of occupation.

b. The authority of the Control Council to formulate policy and procedures and administrative relationships with respect to matters affecting Germany as a whole will be paramount throughout Germany. You will carry out and support in your zone the policies agreed upon in the Control Council. In the absence of such agreed policies you will act in accordance with this and other directives of the Joint Chiefs of Staff.

c. The administration of affairs in Germany shall be directed towards the decentralization of the political and administrative structure and the development of local responsibility. To this end you will encourage autonomy in regional, local, and municipal agencies of German administration. The German economic structure shall also be decentralized. The Control Council may, however, to the minimum extent required for the fulfillment of purposes set forth herein, permit centralized administration or establish central control of (*a*) essential national public services such as railroads, communications, and power, (*b*) finance and foreign affairs, and (*c*) production and distribution of essential commodities.

d. The Control Council should adopt procedures to effectuate, and you will facilitate in your zone, the equitable distribution of essential commodities between the zones. In the absence of a conflicting policy of the Control Council, you may deal directly with one or more zone commanders on matters of special concern to such zones.

e. Pending the formulation in the Control Council of

uniform policies and procedures with respect to inter-
zonal travel and movement of civilians, no civilians shall
be permitted to leave or enter your zone without your
authority, and no Germans within your zone will be permitted to leave Germany except for specific purposes approved by you.

f. The military government personnel in each zone, including those dealing with regional and local branches of
the departments of any central German administrative machinery, shall be selected by authority of the Commander
of that zone except that liaison officers may be furnished
by the Commanders of the other three zones. The respective Commanders-in-Chief shall have exclusive jurisdiction throughout the whole of Germany over the members
of the armed forces under their command and over the
civilians who accompany them.

g. The Control Council should be responsible for facilitating the severance of all governmental and administrative connections between Austria and Germany and the
elimination of German economic influences in Austria.
Every assistance should be given to the Allied Administration in Austria in its efforts to effectuate these purposes.

4. *Basic Objectives of Military Government in Germany:*

a. It should be brought home to the Germans that Germany's ruthless warfare and the fanatical Nazi resistance
have destroyed the German economy and made chaos and
suffering inevitable and that the Germans cannot escape
responsibility for what they have brought upon themselves.

b. Germany will not be occupied for the purpose of
liberation but as a defeated enemy nation. Your aim is not
oppression but to occupy Germany for the purpose of
realizing certain important Allied objectives. In the conduct of your occupation and administration you should be
just, but firm and aloof. You will strongly discourage
fraternization with the German officials and population.

c. The principal Allied objective is to prevent Germany
from ever again becoming a threat to the peace of the
world. Essential steps in the accomplishment of this objective are the elimination of Nazism and militarism in all
their forms, the immediate apprehension of war criminals
for punishment, the industrial disarmament and demili-

tarization of Germany, with continuing control over Germany's capacity to make war, and the preparation for an eventual reconstruction of German political life on a democratic basis.

d. Other Allied objectives are to enforce the program of reparations and restitution, to provide relief for the benefit of countries devastated by Nazi aggression, and to ensure that prisoners of war and displaced persons of the United Nations are cared for and repatriated.

5. *Economic Controls:*

a. As a member of the Control Council and as zone commander, you will be guided by the principle that controls upon the German economy may be imposed to the extent that such controls may be necessary to achieve the objectives enumerated in paragraph 4 above and also as they may be essential to protect the safety and meet the needs of the occupying forces and assure the production and maintenance of goods and services required to prevent starvation or such disease and unrest as would endanger these forces. No action will be taken in execution of the reparations program or otherwise which would tend to support basic living conditions in Germany or in your zone on a higher level than that existing in any one of the neighboring United Nations.

b. In the imposition and maintenance of such controls as may be prescribed by you or the Control Council, German authorities will to the fullest extent practicable be ordered to proclaim and assume administration of such controls. Thus it should be brought home to the German people that the responsibility for the administration of such controls and for any breakdowns in those controls will rest with themselves and German authorities.

6. *Denazification:*

a. A Proclamation dissolving the Nazi Party, its formations, affiliated associations, and supervised organizations, and all Nazi public institutions which were set up as instruments of Party domination, and prohibiting their revival in any form, should be promulgated by the Control Council. You will assure the prompt effectuation of that policy in your zone and will make every effort to prevent the reconstitution of any such organization in underground, disguised or secret form. Responsibility for continuing desirable nonpolitical social services of dissolved Party organizations may be transferred by the Control Council to appropriate central agencies and by you to appropriate local agencies.

b. The laws purporting to establish the political structure of National Socialism and the basis of the Hitler regime and all laws, decrees, and regulations which establish discriminations on grounds of race, nationality, creed, or political opinions should be abrogated by the Control Council. You will render them inoperative in your zone.

c. All members of the Nazi party who have been more than nominal participants in its activities, all active supporters of Nazism or militarism and all other persons hostile to Allied purposes will be removed and excluded from public office and from positions of importance in quasi-public and private enterprises such as (1) civic, economic, and labor organizations, (2) corporations and other organizations in which the German government or subdivisions have a major financial interest, (3) industry, commerce, agriculture, and finance, (4) education, and (5) the press, publishing houses, and other agencies disseminating news and propaganda. Persons are to be treated as more than nominal participants in Party activities and as active supporters of Nazism or militarism when they have (1) held office or otherwise been active at any level from local to national in the party and its subordinate organizations, or in organizations which further militaristic doctrines, (2) authorized or participated affirmatively in any Nazi crimes, racial persecutions, or discriminations, (3) been avowed believers in Nazism or racial and militaristic creeds, or (4) voluntarily given substantial moral or material support or political assistance of any kind to the Nazi Party or Nazi officials and leaders. No such persons shall be retained in any of the categories of employment listed above because of administrative necessity, convenience, or expediency.

d. Property, real and personal, owned or controlled by the Nazi party, its formations, affiliated associations, and supervised organizations, and by all persons subject to arrest under the provisions of paragraph 8 and found within your zone, will be taken under your control pending a decision by the Control Council or higher authority as to its eventual disposition.

e. All archives, monuments, and museums of Nazi inception, or which are devoted to the perpetuation of German militarism, will be taken under your control and their properties held pending decision as to their disposition by the Control Council.

f. You will make special efforts to preserve from destruction and take under your control records, plans, books, documents, papers, files, and scientific, industrial, and other information and data belonging to, or controlled by, the following:

(1) The Central German Government and its subdivisions, German military organizations, organizations engaged in military research, and such other governmental agencies as may be deemed advisable;

(2) The Nazi Party, its formations, affiliated associations, and supervised organizations;

(3) All police organizations, including security and political police;

(4) Important economic organizations and industrial establishments including those controlled by the Nazi Party or its personnel;

(5) Institutes and special bureaus devoting themselves to racial, political, militaristic, or similar research or propaganda.

7. *Demilitarization:*

a. In your zone you will assure that all units of the German armed forces, including para-military organizations, are dissolved as such, and that their personnel are promptly disarmed and controlled. Prior to their final disposition, you will arrest and hold all military personnel who are included under the provisions of paragraph 8.

b. The Control Council should proclaim, and in your zone you will effectuate, the total dissolution of all military and para-military organizations, including the General Staff, the German Officers Corps, the Reserve Corps, and military academies, together with all associations which might serve to keep alive the military tradition in Germany.

c. You will seize or destroy all arms, ammunition, and implements of war and stop the production thereof.

d. You will take proper steps to destroy the German war potential, as set forth elsewhere in this directive.

8. *Suspected War Criminals and Security Arrests:*

a. You will search out, arrest, and hold, pending receipt by you of further instructions as to their disposition, Adolf Hitler, his chief Nazi associates, other war criminals, and all persons who have participated in planning or carrying out Nazi enterprises involving or resulting in atrocities or war crimes.

b. All persons who, if permitted to remain at large would endanger the accomplishment of your objectives will also be arrested and held in custody until trial by an appropriate semi-judicial body to be established by you. The following is a partial list of the categories of persons to be arrested in order to carry out this policy:

(NOTE: *There follows at this point in the directive a detailed list of categories of Nazi war criminals and others who are to be arrested. Some of these have not yet been found. It is considered that to publish the categories at this time would put the individuals concerned on notice and would interfere with their apprehension and punishment, where appropriate. The list of categories is, therefore, withheld from publication for the present.*) [*This note is by the State Department.*]

If in the light of conditions which you encounter in Germany, you believe that it is not immediately feasible to subject certain persons within these categories to this treatment, you should report your reasons and recommendations to your government through the Joint Chiefs of Staff. If you believe it desirable, you may postpone the arrest of those whose cases you have reported, pending a decision communicated to you by the J.C.S. In no event shall any differentiation be made between, or special consideration be accorded to, persons arrested, either as to manner of arrest or conditions of detention, upon the basis of wealth or political, industrial, or other rank or position. In your discretion you may make such exceptions as you deem advisable for intelligence or other military reasons.

9. *Political Activities:*

a. No political activities of any kind shall be countenanced unless authorized by you. You will assure that your military government does not become committed to any political group.

b. You will prohibit the propagation in any form of Nazi, militaristic, or pan-German doctrines.

c. No German parades, military or political, civilian or sports, shall be permitted by you.

d. To the extent that military interests are not prejudiced and subject to the provisions of the three preceding subparagraphs and of paragraph 10, freedom of speech, press, and religious worship will be permitted. Consistent with military necessity, all religious institutions will be respected. . . .

14. *Education:*

a. All educational institutions within your zone except those previously re-established by Allied authority will be closed. The closure of Nazi educational institutions such as Adolf Hitler Schulen, Napolas, and Ordensburgen, and of Nazi organizations within other educational institutions will be permanent.

b. A coordinated system of control over German education and an affirmative program of reorientation will be established designed completely to eliminate Nazi and militaristic doctrines and to encourage the development of democratic ideas.

c. You will permit the reopening of elementary (*Volksschulen*), middle (*Mittelschulen*), and vocational (*Berufsschulen*) schools at the earliest possible date after Nazi personnel has been eliminated. Textbooks and curricula which are not free of Nazi and militaristic doctrine shall not be used. The Control Council should devise programs looking toward the reopening of secondary schools, universities, and other institutions of higher learning. After Nazi features and personnel have been eliminated and pending the formulation of such programs by the Control Council, you may formulate and put into effect an interim program within your zone and in any case may permit the reopening of such institutions and departments which offer training which you consider immediately essential or useful in the administration of military government and the purposes of the occupation.

d. It is not intended that the military government will intervene in questions concerning denominational control

of German schools, or in religious instruction in German
schools, except insofar as may be necessary to insure that
religious instruction and administration of such schools
conform to such Allied regulations as are or may be established pertaining to purging of personnel and curricula. . . .

PART II

ECONOMIC

General Objectives and Methods of Control

16. You will assure that the German economy is ad-
ministered and controlled in such a way as to accomplish
the basic objectives set forth in paragraphs 4 and 5 of
this Directive. Economic controls will be imposed only to
the extent necessary to accomplish these objectives, provided that you will impose controls to the full extent necessary to achieve the industrial disarmament of Germany.
Except as may be necessary to carry out these objectives,
you will take no steps (*a*) looking toward the economic
rehabilitation of Germany, or (*b*) designed to maintain
or strengthen the German economy. . . .

German Standard of Living

21. You will estimate requirements of supplies necessary to prevent starvation or widespread disease or such
civil unrest as would endanger the occupying forces. Such
estimates will be based upon a program whereby the Germans are made responsible for providing for themselves,
out of their own work and resources. You will take all
practicable economic and police measures to assure that
German resources are fully utilized and consumption held
to the minimum in order that imports may be strictly limited and that surpluses may be made available for the
occupying forces and displaced persons and United Nations prisoners of war, and for reparation. You will take
no action that would tend to support basic living standards
in Germany on a higher level than that existing in any
one of the neighboring United Nations and you will take
appropriate measures to ensure that basic living standards
of the German people are not higher than those existing
in any one of the neighboring United Nations when such

measures will contribute to raising the standards of any such nation.

22. You will urge upon the Control Council that uniform ration scales be applied throughout Germany, that essential items be distributed equitably among the zones, that net surpluses be made available for export to Allied countries, and that imports be limited to the net deficits of Germany as a whole.

Labor, Health, and Social Insurance

23. You will permit the self-organization of employees along democratic lines, subject to such safeguards as may be necessary to prevent the perpetuation of Nazi or militarist influence under any guise or the continuation of any group hostile to the objectives and operations of the occupying forces. . . .

Part III

Financial

. . . 50. No extension of credit to Germany or Germans by any foreign person or Government shall be permitted except that the Control Council may in special emergencies grant permission for such extensions of credit.

51. It is not anticipated that you will make credits available to the Reichsbank or any other bank or to any public or private institution. If, in your opinion, such action becomes essential, you may take such emergency actions as you may deem proper, but in any event, you will report the facts to the Control Council.

52. You will maintain such accounts and records as may be necessary to reflect the financial operations of the military government in your zone and you will provide the Control Council with such information as it may require, including information in connection with the use of currency by your forces, any governmental settlements, occupation costs, and other expenditures arising out of operations or activities involving participation of your forces.

43

THE ITALIAN PEACE TREATY, FEBRUARY 10, 1947[51]

Twenty members of the United Nations signed peace treaties with Italy, Bulgaria, Finland, Hungary, and Romania in Paris on February 10, 1947. The ratifications needed to make the pacts effective were deposited on September 15, 1947, in Paris for the Italian Treaty, and in Moscow for the others. The Council of Foreign Ministers (see Document No. 33) *drafted all five documents. At the Council's meetings it was clear "that the main task was not to make peace with Italy and the Balkan Nations, but to make a settlement between the Western Powers and the Soviet Union."*

✦   ✦   ✦

The Union of Soviet Socialist Republics, the United Kingdom of Great Britain and Northern Ireland, the United States of America, China, France, Australia, Belgium, the Byelorussian Soviet Socialist Republic, Brazil, Canada, Czechoslovakia, Ethiopia, Greece, India, the Netherlands, New Zealand, Poland, the Ukrainian Soviet Socialist Republic, the Union of South Africa, and the People's Federal Republic of Yugoslavia, hereinafter referred to as "the Allied and Associated Powers," of the one part, and Italy, of the other part:

Whereas Italy under the Fascist regime became a party to the Tripartite Pact with Germany and Japan, undertook a war of aggression and thereby provoked a state of war with all the Allied and Associated Powers and with other United Nations, and bears her share of responsibility for the war; and

[51] United States, Department of State, Publication No. 2743, *Treaties of Peace with Italy, Bulgaria, Hungary, Romania, and Finland* (*English Versions*), (Government Printing Office, Washington, 1947), pp. 1-110.

Whereas in consequence of the victories of the Allied forces, and with the assistance of the democratic elements of the Italian people, the Fascist regime in Italy was overthrown on July 25, 1943, and Italy, having surrendered unconditionally, signed terms of Armistice on September 3 and 29 of the same year; and

Whereas after the said Armistice Italian armed forces, both of the Government and the Resistance Movement, took an active part in the war against Germany, and Italy declared war on Germany as from October 13, 1943, and thereby became a co-belligerent against Germany; and

Whereas the Allied and Associated Powers and Italy are desirous of concluding a treaty of peace which, in conformity with the principles of justice, will settle questions still outstanding as a result of the events hereinbefore recited and will form the basis of friendly relations between them, thereby enabling the Allied and Associated Powers to support Italy's application to become a member of the United Nations and also to adhere to any convention concluded under the auspices of the United Nations;

Have therefore agreed to declare the cessation of the state of war and for this purpose to conclude the present Treaty of Peace, and have accordingly appointed the undersigned Plenipotentiaries who, after presentation of their full powers, found in good and due form, have agreed on the following provisions: . . .

ARTICLE 14. 1. Italy hereby cedes to Greece in full sovereignty the Dodecanese Islands indicated hereafter, namely Stampalia (Astropalia), Rhodes (Rhodos), Calki (Kharki), Scarpanto, Casos (Casso), Piscopis (Tilos), Misiros (Nisyros), Calimnos (Kalymnos), Leros, Patmos, Lipsos (Lipso), Simi (Symi), Cos (Kos), and Castellorizo, as well as the adjacent islets.

2. These islands shall be and shall remain demilitarized.

3. The procedure and the technical conditions governing the transfer of these islands to Greece will be determined by agreement between the Governments of the United Kingdom and Greece and arrangements shall be made for the withdrawal of foreign troops not later than 90 days from the coming into force of the present Treaty. . . .

ARTICLE 15. Italy shall take all measures necessary to secure to all persons under Italian jurisdiction, without distinction as to race, sex, language, or religion, the enjoyment of human rights and of the fundamental freedoms, including freedom of expression, of press and publication, of religious worship, of political opinion, and of public meeting. . . .

ARTICLE 17. Italy, which, in accordance with Article 30 of the Armistice Agreement, has taken measures to dissolve the Fascist organizations in Italy, shall not permit the resurgence on Italian territory of such organizations, whether political, military, or semi-military, whose purpose it is to deprive the people of their democratic rights. . . .

ARTICLE 21. 1. There is hereby constituted the Free Territory of Trieste, consisting of the area lying between the Adriatic Sea and the boundaries defined in Articles 4 and 22 of the present Treaty. The Free Territory of Trieste is recognized by the Allied and Associated Powers and by Italy, which agree that its integrity and independence shall be assured by the Security Council of the United Nations.

2. Italian sovereignty over the area constituting the Free Territory of Trieste, as above defined, shall be terminated upon the coming into force of the present Treaty.

3. On the termination of Italian sovereignty, the Free Territory of Trieste shall be governed in accordance with an instrument for a provisional regime drafted by the Council of Foreign Ministers and approved by the Security Council. This Instrument shall remain in force until such date as the Security Council shall fix for the coming into force of the Permanent Statute which shall have been approved by it. The Free Territory shall thenceforth be governed by the provisions of such Permanent Statute. The texts of the Permanent Statute and of the Instrument for the Provisional Regime are contained in Annexes VI and VII. . . .

ARTICLE 23. 1. Italy renounces all right and title to the Italian territorial possessions in Africa, i.e. Libya, Eritrea, and Italian Somaliland.

2. Pending their final disposal, the said possessions shall continue under their present administration.

3. The final disposal of these possessions shall be determined jointly by the Governments of the Soviet Union, of the United Kingdom, of the United States of America,

and of France within one year from the coming into force of the present Treaty, in the manner laid down in the joint declaration of February 10, 1947, issued by the said Governments, which is reproduced in Annex XI. . . .

ARTICLE 27. Italy recognizes and undertakes to respect the sovereignty and independence of the State of Albania. . . .

ARTICLE 33. Italy recognizes and undertakes to respect the sovereignty and independence of the State of Ethiopia. . . .

ARTICLE 45. 1. Italy shall take all necessary steps to ensure the apprehension and surrender for trial of:

(a) Persons accused of having committed, ordered, or abetted war crimes and crimes against peace or humanity;

(b) Nationals of any Allied or Associated Power accused of having violated their national law by treason or collaboration with the enemy during the war.

2. At the request of the United Nations Government concerned, Italy shall likewise make available as witnesses persons within its jurisdiction, whose evidence is required for the trial of the persons referred to in paragraph 1 of this Article. . . .

ARTICLE 46. Each of the military, naval, and air clauses of the present Treaty shall remain in force until modified in whole or in part by agreement between the Allied and Associated Powers and Italy or, after Italy becomes a member of the United Nations, by agreement between the Security Council and Italy. . . .

ARTICLE 47. 1. (a) The system of permanent Italian fortifications and military installations along the Franco-Italian frontier, and their armaments, shall be destroyed or removed. . . .

2. The destruction or removal, mentioned in paragraph 1 above, is limited to a distance of 20 kilometers from any point on the frontier as defined by the present Treaty, and shall be completed within one year from the coming into force of the Treaty. . . .

ARTICLE 48. 1. (a) Any permanent Italian fortifications and military installations along the Italo-Yugoslav frontier, and their armaments, shall be destroyed or removed. . . .

ARTICLE 51. Italy shall not possess, construct, or experiment with (i) any atomic weapon, (ii) any self-propelled or guided missiles or apparatus connected with their discharge (other than torpedoes and torpedo-launching gear comprising the normal armament of naval vessels permitted by the present Treaty), (*iii*) any guns with a range of over 30 kilometers, (*iv*) sea mines or torpedoes of non-contact types actuated by influence mechanisms, (*v*) any torpedoes capable of being manned. . . .

ARTICLE 54. The total number of heavy and medium tanks in the Italian armed forces shall not exceed 200.

ARTICLE 55. In no case shall any officer or noncommissioned officer of the former Fascist Militia or of the former Fascist Republican Army be permitted to hold officer's or noncommissioned officer's rank in the Italian Navy, Army, Air Force, or Carabinieri, with the exception of such persons as shall have been exonerated by the appropriate body in accordance with Italian law. . . .

ARTICLE 56. 1. The present Italian Fleet shall be reduced to the units listed in Annex XII A. . . .

ARTICLE 59. 1. No battleship shall be constructed, acquired, or replaced by Italy.

2. No aircraft carrier, submarine or other submersible craft, motor torpedo boat or specialised types of assault craft shall be constructed, acquired, employed, or experimented with by Italy.

3. The total standard displacement of the war vessels, other than battleships, of the Italian Navy, including vessels under construction after the date of launching, shall not exceed 25,000 officers and men. . . .

ARTICLE 61. The Italian Army, including the Frontier Guards, shall be limited to a force of 185,000 combat, service and overhead personnel and 65,000 Carabinieri, though either of the above elements may be varied by 10,000 as long as the total ceiling does not exceed 250,000. The organisation armament of the Italian Ground forces, as well as their deployment throughout Italy, shall be designed to meet only tasks of an internal character, local defence of Italian frontiers and anti-aircraft defence. . . .

ARTICLE 64. 1. The Italian Air Force, including any naval air arm, shall be limited to a force of 200 fighter and reconnaissance aircraft and 150 transport, air-sea rescue, training (school type) and liaison aircraft. These totals include reserve aircraft. All aircraft except for fighter and reconnaissance aircraft shall be unarmed. The organisation and armament of the Italian Air Force, as well as their deployment throughout Italy, shall be designed to meet only tasks of an internal character, local defence of Italian frontiers and defence against air attack.

2. Italy shall not possess or acquire any aircraft designed primarily as bombers with internal bomb-carrying facilities.

ARTICLE 65. 1. The personnel of the Italian Air Force, including any naval air personnel, shall be limited to a total of 25,000 effectives, which shall include combat, service, and overhead personnel. . . .

ARTICLE 73. 1. All armed forces of the Allied and Associated Powers shall be withdrawn from Italy as soon as possible and in any case not later than 90 days from the coming into force of the present Treaty. . . .

ARTICLE 74. A. REPARATION FOR THE UNION OF SOVIET SOCIALIST REPUBLICS

1. Italy shall pay the Soviet Union reparation in the amount of $100,000,000 during a period of seven years from the coming into force of the present Treaty. Deliveries from current industrial production shall not be made during the first two years. . . .

6. The basis of calculation for the settlement provided in this Article will be the United States dollar at its gold parity on July 1, 1946, i.e. $35 for one ounce of gold.

B. REPARATION FOR ALBANIA, ETHIOPIA, GREECE AND YUGOSLAVIA

1. Italy shall pay reparation to the following States:

Albania in the amount of . . . $ 5,000,000
Ethiopia in the amount of . . . $ 25,000,000
Greece in the amount of . . . $105,000,000
Yugoslavia in the amount of . . $125,000,000

These payments shall be made during a period of seven years from the coming into force of the present Treaty. Deliveries from current industrial production shall not be made during the first two years. . . .

ARTICLE 86. 1. For a period not to exceed eighteen months from the coming into force of the present Treaty, the Ambassadors in Rome of the Soviet Union, of the United Kingdom, of the United States of America, and of France, acting in concert, will represent the Allied and

Associated Powers in dealing with the Italian Government in all matters concerning the execution and interpretation of the present Treaty. . . .

ANNEX IV

PROVISIONS AGREED UPON BY THE AUSTRIAN AND ITALIAN GOVERNMENTS ON SEPTEMBER 5, 1946

(Original English text as signed by the two Parties and communicated to the Paris Conference on September 6, 1946)

1. German-speaking inhabitants of the Bolzano Province and of the neighbouring bilingual townships of the Trento Province will be assured complete equality of rights with the Italian-speaking inhabitants, within the framework of special provisions to safeguard the ethnical character and the cultural and economic development of the German-speaking element.

In accordance with legislation already enacted or awaiting enactment the said German-speaking citizens will be granted in particular:

(a) elementary and secondary teaching in the mother tongue;

(b) parification of the German and Italian languages in public offices and official documents, as well as in bilingual topographic naming;

(c) the right to re-establish German family names which were Italianized in recent years;

(d) equality of rights as regards the entering upon public offices, with a view to reaching a more appropriate proportion of employment between the two ethnical groups. . . .

ANNEX XI

JOINT DECLARATION BY THE GOVERNMENTS OF THE SOVIET UNION, OF THE UNITED KINGDOM, OF THE UNITED STATES OF AMERICA AND OF FRANCE CONCERNING ITALIAN TERRITORIAL POSSESSIONS IN AFRICA

(See Article 23)

1. The Governments of the Union of Soviet Socialist Republics, of the United Kingdom of Great Britain and

Northern Ireland, of the United States of America, and of France agree that they will, within one year from the coming into force of the Treaty of Peace with Italy bearing the date of February 10, 1947, jointly determine the final disposal of Italy's territorial possessions in Africa, to which, in accordance with Article 23 of the Treaty, Italy renounces all right and title.

2. The final disposal of the territories concerned and the appropriate adjustment of their boundaries shall be made by the Four Powers in the light of the wishes and welfare of the inhabitants and the interests of peace and security, taking into consideration the views of other interested Governments. . . .

In faith whereof the undersigned Plenipotentiaries have signed the present Treaty and have affixed thereto their seals.

Done in the city of Paris in the French, English, Russian, and Italian languages this tenth day of February, One Thousand Nine Hundred Forty-Seven.

[Signatures]

— 44 —

THE JAPANESE PEACE TREATY, SEPTEMBER 8, 1951 [52]

A Japanese peace treaty was delayed more than six years after V-J Day largely because of United States-Soviet disagreements. Moscow wanted the document drafted by herself, the United States, Great Britain, and

[52] United States, Department of State, Publication No. 4561, *Treaty of Peace with Japan Signed at San Francisco, September 8, 1951, with Related Documents* (Government Printing Office, Washington, 1952).

*China, with a veto right for each. Washington wanted a
much broader representation of powers with no veto and
a two-thirds majority for decisions. Eventually, Washington decided to seek a non-punitive settlement (with or
without Soviet participation) that would recreate a viable
Japan protected, during its disarmed period, against foreign aggression. John Foster Dulles, as adviser to the
Department of State, visited many countries to discuss
treaty terms, and then two successive drafts were circu-
lated for suggestions. At last, on September 8, 1951, a
peace pact was signed in San Francisco by forty-eight nations and Japan. Czechoslovakia, Poland, and the U.S.S.R.
refused to sign the treaty. (India, Burma, and Yugoslavia
had declined invitations to attend the conference.) The
treaty was proclaimed on April 28, 1952, on which day
Washington and Tokyo also signed a security agreement
permitting the stationing of United States troops on Japanese soil "so as to deter armed attack" on the island empire while "irresponsible militarism" still was rampant.
By the end of 1957 most of the United States forces had
been withdrawn from Japan.*

✓   ✓   ✓

Whereas the Allied Powers and Japan are resolved that
henceforth their relations shall be those of nations which,
as sovereign equals, cooperate in friendly association to
promote their common welfare and to maintain international peace and security, and are therefore desirous of
concluding a Treaty of Peace which will settle questions
still outstanding as a result of the existence of a state of
war between them;

Whereas Japan for its part declares its intention to apply
for membership in the United Nations and in all circumstances to conform to the principles of the Charter of the
United Nations; to strive to realize the objectives of the
Universal Declaration of Human Rights; to seek to create
within Japan conditions of stability and well-being as defined in Articles 55 and 56 of the Charter of the United
Nations and already initiated by post-surrender Japanese
legislation; and in public and private trade and commerce
to conform to internationally accepted fair practices;

Whereas the Allied Powers welcome the intentions of
Japan set out in the foregoing paragraph;

The Allied Powers and Japan have therefore determined to conclude the present Treaty of Peace, and have accordingly appointed the undersigned Plenipotentiaries, who, after presentation of their full powers, found in good and due form, have agreed on the following provisions: . . .

ARTICLE 1. (a) The state of war between Japan and each of the Allied Powers is terminated as from the date on which the present Treaty comes into force between Japan and the Allied Power concerned as provided for in Article 23.

(b) The Allied Powers recognize the full sovereignty of the Japanese people over Japan and its territorial waters. . . .

ARTICLE 2. (a) Japan, recognizing the independence of Korea, renounces all right, title, and claim to Korea, including the islands of Quelpart, Port Hamilton, and Dagelet.

(b) Japan renounces all right, title, and claim to Formosa and the Pescadores.

(c) Japan renounces all right, title, and claim to the Kurile Islands, and to that portion of Sakhalin and the islands adjacent to it over which Japan acquired sovereignty as a consequence of the Treaty of Portsmouth of September 5, 1905.

(d) Japan renounces all right, title, and claim in connection with the League of Nations Mandate System, and accepts the action of the United Nations Security Council of April 2, 1947, extending the trusteeship system to the Pacific Islands formerly under mandate to Japan.

(e) Japan renounces all claim to any right or title or to interest in connection with any part of the Antarctic area, whether deriving from the activities of Japanese nationals or otherwise.

(f) Japan renounces all right, title, and claim to the Spratly Islands and to the Paracel Islands.

ARTICLE 3. Japan will concur in any proposal of the United States to the United Nations to place under its trusteeship system, with the United States as the sole administering authority, Nansei Shoto south of 29° north latitude (including Ryukyu Islands and the Daito Islands), Nanpo Shoto south of Sofu Gan (including the Bonin Islands, Rosario Island, and the Volcano Islands) and Parece Vela and Marcus Island. Pending the making

of such a proposal and affirmative action thereon, the United States will have the right to exercise all and any powers of administration, legislation, and jurisdiction over the territory and inhabitants of these islands, including their territorial waters. . . .

ARTICLE 5. (a) Japan accepts the obligations set forth in Article 2 of the Charter of the United Nations, and in particular the obligations

(i) to settle its international disputes by peaceful means in such a manner that international peace and security, and justice, are not endangered;

(ii) to refrain in its international relations from the threat or use of force against the territorial integrity or political independence of any State or in any other manner inconsistent with the Purposes of the United Nations;

(iii) to give the United Nations every assistance in any action it takes in accordance with the Charter and to refrain from giving assistance to any State against which the United Nations may take preventive or enforcement action. . . .

ARTICLE 10. Japan renounces all special rights and interests in China, including all benefits and privileges resulting from the provisions of the final Protocol signed at Peking on September 7, 1901, and all annexes, notes, and documents supplementary thereto, and agrees to the abrogation in respect to Japan of the said protocol, annexes, notes, and documents.

ARTICLE 11. Japan accepts the judgments of the International Military Tribunal for the Far East and of other Allied War Crimes Courts both within and outside Japan, and will carry out the sentences imposed thereby upon Japanese nationals imprisoned in Japan. The power to grant clemency, to reduce sentences, and to parole with respect to such prisoners may not be exercised except on the decision of the Government or Governments which imposed the sentence in each instance, and on the recommendation of Japan. In the case of persons sentenced by the International Military Tribunal for the Far East, such power may not be exercised except on the decision of a majority of the Governments represented on the Tribunal, and on the recommendation of Japan. . . .

ARTICLE 14. (a) It is recognized that Japan should pay reparations to the Allied Powers for the damage and

suffering caused by it during the war. Nevertheless it is also recognized that the resources of Japan are not presently sufficient, if it is to maintain a viable economy, to make complete reparation for all such damage and suffering and at the same time meet its other obligations.

Therefore,

1. Japan will promptly enter into negotiations with Allied Powers so desiring, whose present territories were occupied by Japanese forces and damaged by Japan, with a view to assisting to compensate those countries for the cost of repairing the damage done, by making available the services of the Japanese people in production, salvaging, and other work for the Allied Powers in question. Such arrangements shall avoid the imposition of additional liabilities on other Allied Powers, and, where the manufacturing of raw materials is called for, they shall be supplied by the Allied Powers in question, so as not to throw any foreign exchange burden upon Japan. . . .

ARTICLE 23. (a) The present Treaty shall be ratified by the States which sign it, including Japan, and will come into force for all the States which have then ratified it, when instruments of ratification have been deposited by Japan and by a majority, including the United States of America as the principal occupying Power, of the following States, namely Australia, Canada, Ceylon, France, Indonesia, the Kingdom of the Netherlands, New Zealand, Pakistan, the Republic of the Philippines, the United Kingdom of Great Britain and Northern Ireland, and the United States of America. The present Treaty shall come into force for each State which subsequently ratifies it, on the date of the deposit of its instrument of ratification. . . .

ARTICLE 27. The present Treaty shall be deposited in the archives of the Government of the United States of America which shall furnish each signatory State with a certified copy thereof.

In Faith Whereof the undersigned Plenipotentiaries have signed the present Treaty.

Done at the city of San Francisco this eighth day of September, 1951, in the English, French, and Spanish languages, all being equally authentic, and in the Japanese language.

— 45 —

END OF WAR WITH GERMANY, OCTOBER 19, 1951 [53]

The continuing unwillingness of the Soviet Union to permit a reunification of West and East Germany except along lines virtually guaranteeing a Communist dictatorship, and the orderly political and economic progress in the western part of the country known as the Federal Republic of Germany, led the Western Allies in September, 1950 to declare their intention of ending the state of war with the Germans. The occupation forces would remain, so as to protect the free world, and the Federal Republic and western Berlin in particular, against possible Soviet aggression. Despite strenuous objections from Moscow, Great Britain and France on July 9, 1951, and the United States by joint resolution of Congress on October 19, 1951, ended the state of war with "the Government of Germany." This act did not limit or otherwise affect the rights of the United States as an occupying power. (United States, 82nd Congress, 1st Session, 1951, House Miscellaneous Reports, vol. III, No. 705, p. 8). A Bonn Convention of May 26, 1952, signed by the Western Allies and the Federal Republic, extended to the latter as much sovereignty as was possible for a divided Germany with foreign troops on its soil. Letters accompanying a "Treaty of Friendship, Commerce, and Navigation" between the United States and the Bonn Government, effective on July 14, 1956, still provided that "the present special position of the United States of America and its personnel in Germany shall not be affected by the aforesaid treaty."

Public Law 181

JOINT RESOLUTION

[53] *United States Statutes at Large* (Government Printing Office, Washington, 1952), LXV, 451.

To terminate the state of war between the United States and the Government of Germany.

Resolved by the Senate and House of Representatives of the United States of America in Congress assembled, That the state of war declared to exist between the United States and the Government of Germany by the joint resolution of Congress approved December 11, 1941, is hereby terminated and such termination shall take effect on the date of enactment of this resolution: *Provided, however,* That notwithstanding this resolution and any proclamation issued by the President pursuant thereto, any property or interest which prior to January 1, 1947, was subject to vesting or seizure under the provisions of the Trading With the Enemy Act of October 6, 1917 (40 Stat. 411), as amended, or which has heretofore been vested or seized under that Act, including accruals to or proceeds of any such property or interest, shall continue to be subject to the provisions of that Act in the same manner and to the same extent as if this resolution had not been adopted and such proclamation had not been issued. Nothing herein and nothing in such proclamation shall alter the status, as it existed immediately prior hereto, under that Act, of Germany or of any person with respect to any such property or interest.

Approved October 19, 1951

— 46 —

THE AUSTRIAN PEACE TREATY, MAY 15 1955 [54]

Negotiations for a peace treaty with Austria dragged on for many years after the Italian and Balkan treaties were

[54] United States, Department of State, *United States Treaties and Other International Agreements* (Government Printing Office, Washington, 1956), VI, pt. 2, 1955, 2408-2442.

*completed. The Western Powers insisted that the peace
be in accord with the Declaration on Austria of the Moscow Conference of 1943. (See Document No. 29.) The
Soviet Union wanted to give an important piece of Austria
to Yugoslavia (along with $150,000,000 in "reparation")
and demanded economic provisions which in effect would
have made much of Austria a part of the Soviet Union by
giving the latter ownership of the most important section
of Austrian economy and the right to operate this free
from control by Austrian law. Moscow also kept delaying
matters because Article 22 of the 1947 peace treaty with
Hungary allowed the Soviet Union to keep soldiers in
Hungary as long as she wished to maintain direct lines
of communication between the Soviet Army and the Soviet
Zone of Occupation in Austria. In other words, by remaining in Austria, Russia also legally could remain in Hungary! At last, however, a "State Treaty for the Re-establishment of an Independent and Democratic Austria" was
signed in Vienna on May 15, 1955, and went into force
on July 27, 1955.*

✓   ✓   ✓

PREAMBLE

The Union of Soviet Socialist Republics, the United
Kingdom of Great Britain and Northern Ireland, the
United States of America, and France, hereinafter referred
to as "the Allied and Associated Powers," of the one part
and Austria, of the other part;

Whereas on 13th March, 1938, Hitlerite Germany annexed Austria by force and incorporated its territory in
the German Reich;

Whereas in the Moscow Declaration published on 1st
November, 1943, the Governments of the Union of Soviet
Socialist Republics, the United Kingdom and the United
States of America declared that they regarded the annexation of Austria by Germany on 13th March, 1938, as null
and void and affirmed their wish to see Austria re-established as a free and independent State, and the French
Committee of National Liberation made a similar declaration on 16th November, 1943;

Whereas as a result of the Allied victory Austria was
liberated from the domination of Hitlerite Germany;

Whereas the Allied and Associated Powers, and Austria, taking into account the importance of the efforts which the Austrian people themselves have made and will have to continue to make for the restoration and democratic reconstruction of their country, desire to conclude a treaty re-establishing Austria as a free, independent, and democratic State, thus contributing to the restoration of peace in Europe;

Whereas the Allied and Associated Powers desire by means of the present Treaty to settle in accordance with the principles of justice all questions which are still outstanding in connection with the events referred to above, including the annexation of Austria by Hitlerite Germany and participation of Austria in the war as an integral part of Germany; and

Whereas the Allied and Associated Powers and Austria are desirous for these purposes of concluding the present Treaty to serve as the basis of friendly relations between them, thereby enabling the Allied and Associated Powers to support Austria's application for admission to the United Nations Organization;

Have therefore appointed the undersigned Plenipotentiaries who, after presentation of their full powers, found in good and due form, have agreed on the following provisions: . . .

ARTICLE 1. The Allied and Associated Powers recognize that Austria is re-established as a sovereign, independent, and democratic State.

ARTICLE 2. The Allied and Associated Powers declare that they will respect the independence and territorial integrity of Austria as established under the present Treaty. . . .

ARTICLE 5. The frontiers of Austria shall be those existing on 1st January, 1938. . . .

ARTICLE 8. Austria shall have a democratic government based on elections by secret ballot and shall guarantee to all citizens free, equal, and universal suffrage, as well as the right to be elected to public office without discrimination as to race, sex, language, religion, or political opinion.

ARTICLE 9. 1. Austria shall complete the measures, already begun by the enactment of appropriate legislation approved by the Allied Commission for Austria, to destroy the National Socialist Party and its affiliated and supervised organizations, including political, military, and para-military organizations, on Austrian territory. Austria shall also continue the efforts to eliminate from Austrian political, economic, and cultural life all traces of Nazism, to ensure that the above-mentioned organizations are not revived in any form, and to prevent all Nazi and militarist activity and propaganda in Austria.

2. Austria undertakes to dissolve all Fascist-type organizations existing on its territory, political, military, and para-military, and likewise any other organizations carrying on activities hostile to any United Nation or which intend to deprive the people of their democratic rights. . . .

ARTICLE 13. 1. Austria shall not possess, construct, or experiment with—a) Any atomic weapon, b) any other major weapon adaptable now or in the future to mass destruction and defined as such by the appropriate organ of the United Nations, c) any self-propelled or guided missile or torpedoes, or apparatus connected with their discharge or control, d) sea mines, e) torpedoes capable of being manned, f) submarines or other submersible craft, g) motor torpedo boats, h) specialized types of assault craft, i) guns with a range of more than 30 kilometers, j) asphyxiating, vesicant, or poisonous materials or biological substances in quantities greater than, or of types other than, are required for legitimate civil purposes, or any apparatus designed to produce, project, or spread such materials or substances for war purposes. . . .

ARTICLE 20. 1. The Agreement on the Machinery of Control in Austria of 28th June, 1946 shall terminate on the coming into force of the present Treaty.

2. On the coming into force of the present Treaty, the Inter-Allied Command established under paragraph 4 of the Agreement on Zones of Occupation in Austria and the Administration of the City of Vienna of 9th July, 1945, shall cease to exercise any functions with respect to the administration of the City of Vienna. The Agreement on Zones of Occupation of Austria shall terminate upon completion of the withdrawal from Austria of the forces of the Allied and Associated Powers in accordance with paragraph 3 of the present Article.

3. The forces of the Allied and Associated Powers and

members of the Allied Commission for Austria shall be withdrawn from Austria within ninety days from the coming into force of the present Treaty, and insofar as possible not later than 31st December, 1955. . . .

ARTICLE 21. No reparation shall be exacted from Austria arising out of the existence of a state of war in Europe after 1st September, 1939.

ARTICLE 22. The Soviet Union, the United Kingdom, the United States of America, and France have the right to dispose of all German assets in Austria in accordance with the Protocol of the Berlin Conference of 2nd August, 1945.

1. The Soviet Union shall receive for a period of validity of thirty years concessions to oil fields equivalent to 60 per cent of the extraction of oil in Austria for 1947, as well as property rights to all buildings, constructions, equipment, and other property belonging to these oil fields, in accordance with list No. 1 and map No. 1 annexed to the Treaty.

2. The Soviet Union shall receive concessions to 60 per cent of all exploration areas located in Eastern Austria that are German assets to which the Soviet Union is entitled in conformity with the Potsdam Agreement and which are in its possession at the present time, in accordance with list No. 2 and map No. 2 annexed to the Treaty.

The Soviet Union shall have the right to carry out explorations on the exploration areas mentioned in the present paragraph for 8 years and to subsequent extraction of oil for a period of 25 years beginning from the moment of the discovery of oil.

3. The Soviet Union shall receive oil refineries having a total annual production capacity of 420,000 tons of crude oil, in accordance with list No. 3.

4. The Soviet Union shall receive those undertakings concerned in the distribution of oil products which are at its disposal, in accordance with list No. 4.

5. The Soviet Union shall receive the assets of the Danube Shipping Company (D.D.S.G.), located in Hungary, Roumania and Bulgaria; and, likewise, in accordance with list No. 5, 100 per cent of the assets of the Danube Shipping Company located in Eastern Austria.

6. The Soviet Union shall transfer to Austria property,

rights, and interests held or claimed as German assets, together with existing equipment, and shall also transfer war industrial enterprises, together with existing equipment, houses, and similar immovable property, including plots of land, located in Austria and held or claimed as war booty with the exception of the assets mentioned in paragraphs 1, 2, 3, 4, and 5 of the present Article. Austria for its part undertakes to pay the Soviet Union 150,000,000 United States dollars in freely convertible currency within a period of 6 years. . . .

7. Legal Position of Assets:

(a) All former German assets which have become the property of the Soviet Union in accordance with paragraphs 1, 2, 3, 4, and 5 of the present Article shall, as the general rule, remain under Austrian jurisdiction and, in conformity with this, Austrian legislation shall apply to them. . . .

ARTICLE 23. 1. From the date of the coming into force of the present Treaty the property in Germany of the Austrian Government or of Austrian nationals, including property forcibly removed from Austrian territory to Germany after 12th March, 1938 shall be returned to its owners. This provision shall not apply to the property of war criminals or persons who have been subjected to the penalties of denazification measures; such property shall be placed at the disposal of the Austrian Government if it has not been subjected to blocking or confiscation in accordance with the laws or ordinances in force in Germany after 8th May, 1945. . . .

ARTICLE 31. Navigation on the Danube shall be free and open for the nationals, vessels of commerce, and goods of all States, on a footing of equality in regard to port and navigation charges and conditions for merchant shipping. The foregoing shall not apply to traffic between ports of the same State. . . .

ARTICLE 38. 1. The present Treaty, of which the Russian, English, French, and German texts are authentic, shall be ratified. It shall come into force immediately upon deposit of instruments of ratification by the Union of Soviet Socialist Republics, by the United Kingdom of Great Britain and Northern Ireland, by the United States of America, and by France of the one part and by Austria of the other part. The instruments of ratification shall, in the shortest time possible, be deposited with the Government of the Union of Soviet Socialist Republics.

2. With respect to each Allied and Associated Power whose instrument of ratification is thereafter deposited, the Treaty shall come into force upon the date of deposit. The present Treaty shall be deposited in the archives of the Government of the Union of Soviet Socialist Republics, which shall furnish certified copies to each of the signatory and acceding States.

— 47 —

THE TRIAL AND PUNISHMENT OF "WAR CRIMINALS," AUGUST 9, 1945 [55]

The United States, Great Britain, France, and the Soviet Union signed a London agreement on August 8, 1945, concerning the prosecution of "war criminals" and the establishment of an International Military Tribunal to judge the prominent defendants whose offences had "no particular geographic location." Twenty-two major Nazi defendants were tried in Nuremberg; the less important prisoners were tried in the several occupation zones. In the United States Zone, for example, 185 individuals were indicted and the legal proceedings stretched from October 1946–April 1949.

✓   ✓   ✓

[55] *A* is from United States, Office of United States Chief of Counsel for Prosecution of Axis Criminality, *Nazi Conspiracy and Aggression,* 8 vols. and 2 suppl. vols. (Government Printing Office, Washington, 1946-1948), I, 1-3; *B* is from United States, Office of United States Chief of Counsel for Prosecution for Axis Criminality, *Nazi Conspiracy and Aggression: Opinion and Judgment* (Government Printing Office, Washington, 1947), pp. 189-190.

A

AGREEMENT BY THE GOVERNMENT OF THE UNITED STATES OF AMERICA, THE PROVISIONAL GOVERNMENT OF THE FRENCH REPUBLIC, THE GOVERNMENT OF THE UNITED KINGDOM OF GREAT BRITAIN AND NORTHERN IRELAND, AND THE GOVERNMENT OF THE UNION OF SOVIET SOCIALIST REPUBLICS FOR THE PROSECUTION AND PUNISHMENT OF THE MAJOR WAR CRIMINALS OF THE EUROPEAN AXIS

Whereas the United Nations have from time to time made declarations of their intention that War Criminals shall be brought to justice;

And whereas the Moscow Declaration of the 30th October, 1943 [*see Document No. 29*] on German atrocities in Occupied Europe stated that those German Officers and men and members of the Nazi Party who have been responsible for, or have taken a consenting part in, atrocities and crimes will be sent back to the countries in which their abominable deeds were done in order that they may be judged and punished according to the laws of these liberated countries and of the free Governments that will be created therein;

And whereas this Declaration was stated to be without prejudice to the case of major criminals whose offenses have no particular geographic location and who will be punished by the joint decision of the Governments of the Allies;

Now therefore the Government of the United States of America, the Provisional Government of the French Republic, the Government of the United Kingdom of Great Britain and Northern Ireland, and the Government of the Union of Soviet Socialist Republics (hereinafter called "the Signatories") acting in the interests of all the United Nations and by their representatives duly authorized thereto have concluded this Agreement.

ARTICLE 1. There shall be established after consultation with the Control Council for Germany an International Military Tribunal for the trial of war criminals whose offenses have no particular geographical location whether they be accused individually or in their capacity as members of organizations or groups or in both capacities.

ARTICLE 2. The constitution, jurisdiction, and functions of the International Military Tribunal shall be those set out in the Charter annexed to this Agreement, which Charter shall form an integral part of this Agreement.

ARTICLE 3. Each of the Signatories shall take the necessary steps to make available for the investigation of the charges and trial the major war criminals detained by them who are to be tried by the International Military Tribunal. The Signatories shall also use their best endeavors to make available for investigation of the charges against, and the trial before, the International Military Tribunal such of the major war criminals as are not in the territories of any of the Signatories.

ARTICLE 4. Nothing in this Agreement shall prejudice the provisions established by the Moscow Declaration concerning the return of war criminals to the countries where they committed their crimes.

ARTICLE 5. Any Government of the United Nations may adhere to this Agreement by notice given through the diplomatic channel to the Government of the United Kingdom, who shall inform the other signatory and adhering Governments of each such adherence.

ARTICLE 6. Nothing in this Agreement shall prejudice the jurisdiction or the powers of any national or occupation court established or to be established in any allied territory or in Germany for the trial of war criminals.

ARTICLE 7. This Agreement shall come into force on the day of signature and shall remain in force for the period of one year and shall continue thereafter, subject to the right of any Signatory to give, through the diplomatic channel, one month's notice of intention to terminate it. Such termination shall not prejudice any proceedings already taken or any findings already made in pursuance of this Agreement.

IN WITNESS WHEREOF the Undersigned have signed the present Agreement.

Done in quadruplicate in London this 8th day of August, 1945, each in English, French, and Russian, and each text to have equal authenticity.

B

THE SENTENCES

In accordance with Article 27 of the Charter, the President of the International Military Tribunal, at its concluding session of 1 October, 1946, pronounced sentence on the defendants convicted on the indictment:

Defendant Hermann Wilhelm Goering, on the counts of the indictment on which you have been convicted, the International Military Tribunal sentences you to death by hanging.

Defendant Rudolf Hess, on the counts of the indictment on which you have been convicted, the Tribunal sentences you to imprisonment for life.

Defendant Joachim von Ribbentrop, on the counts of the indictment on which you have been convicted, the Tribunal sentences you to death by hanging.

Defendant Wilhelm Keitel, on the counts of the indictment on which you have been convicted, the Tribunal sentences you to death by hanging.

Defendant Ernst Kaltenbrunner, on the counts of the indictment on which you have been convicted, the Tribunal sentences you to death by hanging.

Defendant Alfred Rosenberg, on the counts of the indictment on which you have been convicted, the Tribunal sentences you to death by hanging.

Defendant Hans Frank, on the counts of the indictment on which you have been convicted, the Tribunal sentences you to death by hanging.

Defendant Wilhelm Frick, on the counts of the indictment on which you have been convicted, the Tribunal sentences you to death by hanging.

Defendant Julius Streicher, on the count of the indictment on which you have been convicted, the Tribunal sentences you to death by hanging.

Defendant Walter Funk, on the counts of the indictment on which you have been convicted, the Tribunal sentences you to imprisonment for life.

Defendant Karl Doenitz, on the counts of the indictment on which you have been convicted, the Tribunal sentences you to 10 years' imprisonment.

Defendant Erich Raeder, on the counts of the indictment on which you have been convicted, the Tribunal sentences you to imprisonment for life.

Defendant Baldur von Schirach, on the count of the indictment on which you have been convicted, the Tribunal sentences you to 20 years' imprisonment.

Defendant Fritz Sauckel, on the counts of the indictment on which you have been convicted, the Tribunal sentences you to death by hanging.

Defendant Alfred Jodl, on the counts of the indictment on which you have been convicted, the Tribunal sentences you to death by hanging.

Defendant Arthur Seyss-Inquart, on the counts of the indictment on which you have been convicted, the Tribunal sentences you to death by hanging.

Defendant Albert Speer, on the counts of the indictment on which you have been convicted, the Tribunal sentences you to 20 years' imprisonment.

Defendant Konstantin von Neurath, on the counts of the indictment on which you have been convicted, the Tribunal sentences you to 15 years' imprisonment.

The Tribunal sentences the Defendant Martin Bormann, on the counts of the indictment on which he has been convicted, to death by hanging. [*In absentia.*] [56]

[56] Martin Bormann could not be found after the war.